CF ALIVE

MAKING COLDFUSION MODERN, VIBRANT AND SECURE

By Michaela Light

WWIT for you to get amazing results from the tools in this book, expand your ColdFusion skills and share them openly in the CF community?

Table of Contents

Introduction

The CF Alive Roadmap

Don't listen to what some people say. I'm here to show you that ColdFusion is a vibrant and modern language for complex, data-driven enterprise apps. While some companies have abandoned ColdFusion as dying, more visionary dev teams have embraced CF. Learn how they are making it the most modern, secure and state-of-the-art web development ecosystem. Bar none.

What is this book about?

I will explain how to:

- **Modernize** your legacy CF apps with 14 best practices for easy-to-maintain apps
- Discover 27 **state-of-the-art tools** from my hand-picked list that will make you more efficient at CF development
- Inspire others developers and young programmers with our **proven 21 outreach** methods
- Learn 8 keys to improve CF **Marketing** and be proud of using ColdFusion
- **Contribute** to making CF more alive

This book helps you learn how to make your CF modern, vibrant and secure. Let's look at each of those in more detail.

Modern

Let's be real. CF is an older programming language originally created in 1995. (Mind you, Bjarne Stroustrup created C++ in 1985). While CF has regular upgrades (currently every 2 years), there are some people who see it as old and legacy. I am going to deconstruct this false view and show you how CF is a state-of-the-art language. I will examine 14 best practices in Chapter 1,"Modernization", and then in Chapter 2, "State of the Art Tools", I will guide you personally through 27 tools that modernize CF as a language and will modernize your CF development processes too.

> *"I've been in ColdFusion for over 20 years. I started in '97,*
> *and I've stuck with it throughout."*
>
> - Charlie Arehart, Veteran server troubleshooter CArehart.org

From CF Alive episode, "013 Are spiders eating your servers? The impact of their unexpected load and how to counter it with Charlie Arehart"

Note: you can find all the linked podcasts, articles and tools from this book at: www.teratech.com/CFAliveBookLinks

If by some chance you are new to ColdFusion, let me give you a quick overview. CF it is a development platform for creating modern web applications on the JVM. The CFML language has tags that resemble HTML syntax for templating HTML and a script language that resembles JavaScript syntax for writing business logic. It is designed to be powerful, expressive and easy to with which to get started coding. Many features are built into ColdFusion that require add-ons for other languages.

A note on names

In this book I use several names for ColdFusion and its different variants.

- ColdFusion and CF - any version of the ColdFusion server and language by any manufacturer

- CFML (ColdFusion Markup Language) is the correct name for the ColdFusion language by any manufacturer
- ACF (Adobe ColdFusion) - the commercial version of ColdFusion from Adobe
- Lucee or Lucee CFML - the free open source version of ColdFusion from the Lucee organization

Vibrant

Some CFers have become a bit burnt out; maybe they are bored, and they have become a little cynical of CF and their jobs. They don't want to learn new stuff, some some are afraid to even try.

We want to be young again and learn new coding methods and features for the first time. Let's recapture the excitement of coding in CF again and know that it is the "in thing" to do.

In Chapter 3, "Outreach" and Chapter 4, "Marketing" I look at how CF and the CF community can be more vibrant and alive. From education to developer outreach, education and conferences to PR and marketing, I share ideas with you that include both corporate actions and grass-roots ideas that you can do yourself to strengthen your involvement in what you may discover is a surprisingly vibrant community.

> *"...the phrase was, "This is not your father's Oldsmobile." Well the ColdFusion I'm using isn't my father's ColdFusion. Although technically that would be me, because I have a son who's a full-time professional ColdFusion developer also. But he's not using the ColdFusion I started with. This is a very mature feature."*
>
> - John Farrar, CEO, SOSensible Group

From CF Alive episode, "018 VUE More With Less, with John Farrar"

Secure

Hacking is on the increase and at times CF has been accused of being insecure. I am going to help you look at the facts and discover that CF is actually the *most secure* web language. In Chapter 1, "Modernization", I examine how you can make your CF apps even more secure with special technique and tools.

> *"...why would you not reach for something that's tried and true and innovative and you can make a great product with?"*
>
> - Nathaniel Francis, Works at Computer Know How

From CF Alive episode, "008 The Best REST You've ever Had: ColdBox REST with Nathaniel Francis"

Who is this book for?

I wrote this book for CIOs at a company that uses ColdFusion and a CF developers. I speak with hundreds of CIOs and CF developers every year. Here are some of the things they share with me:

CIOs

They are the CIO (Chief Information Officer) at an organization that uses CF. (I include people with job titles of CTO (Chief Technology Officer), Director of IT (Information Technology) or PM (Project Manager) in this category as well.

CIOs commonly share with me the following concerns about CF:

- Perhaps they are concerned about being seen backing a losing technology and they need to look strong in the C-suite. (The C-suite includes the CEO (Chief Executive Officer), COO (Chief Operating Officer), CFO (Chief Financial Officer), CMO (Chief Marketing Officer), etc.)

- They may have had a perception that CF is dying, is legacy and is not modern or "cool."
- They might be anxious that it is difficult to hire good CF developers, or that modernizing a CF app will take money away from other priorities that are "sexier".
  - Fear that modernizing applications and servers is a potential minefield and is not glamorous. They may be concerned that there is no big payoff with sticking with CF.
  - They have so many servers unpatched/un-updated; so much orphaned code.
- They have to allocate your budget across the company's systems and initiatives.
- They are concerned about efficiency, cost savings, are they using the right technology, are they at risk for security or compliance issues.

What they want:

- Need to be reassured that CF continues to evolve and can handle their issues, especially security.
- That they can continue to use CF, so that they don't have to pull money from other projects. The CF systems are basically working well, and it is a solid language.
- That they will always be able to hire quality CF developers. Or get help from a vendor who knows what they are doing and has quality CF team on staff.
- And that they can efficiently onboard new CF developers to their team and their code base / development process.
- They want to create new strategic initiatives that give them a high profile in the company. For their next job, they might need to move to a bigger company; and need to show successful projects. They need to have "sexy" projects to talk about.
- They want to be less stressed and less in firefighting mode.

CF developers

They are a ColdFusion developer. Either at a company or freelance.

Developers commonly share with me the following concerns about CF:

- They are concerned that there is a perception that CF is dying, is legacy, is not a modern or "cool" language
- They might be anxious that they have picked the wrong language to use, that using CF is bad for their career, and will make it hard to get new job. They are also concerned that if their company modernizes and gets rid of CF, that they will have a hard time finding a new job.
- They may have chosen to stay in CF even when they heard the dying/legacy chatter. Even though some other developers have moved on to other languages, including some high profile folks.
- Perhaps they felt resigned to staying with CF and now feel apathetic about it. They have encountered "language shame."
  - But they do recognize that they have been tenacious to hang on and wished that they were more proud of using CF. Perhaps even become a CF ambassador!
- They are very busy day-to-day, maybe lower ambition, don't have a strong drive (or the time) to learn something to learn new CF features or even a new language.
- They feel a bit burnt out, worn out, a little cynical
  - Staying in comfort zone
  - Hoping the language stays around for long enough for them to retire
  - They are afraid to try something else.

What they want:

- To be doing cool coding, learning new tech, being perceived as cool or with the "in crowd"
- They want to grow personally, and to enjoy what they are working on

- They like being acknowledged for saving the day from time to time
- They want to use a language that hey are proud of and that is modern and alive
- That they are part of a vibrant and helpful CF community that does not have negativity and backbiting.
- To be one of the masters of CF, in demand and being interviewed on the CF Alive podcast.

The State of the ColdFusion Ecosystem

In the State of CF Union Survey 2018 (Amazing Final Results & Analysis) I asked:

What aspects of CF are preventing you or your company from embracing CF?

The top concern, which was given by 72% of the participants, say that is is because CF is seen as dying/legacy.

I am committed to changing his perception in both this book and the CF Alive podcast!

> *"Eric: What's it like being a new ColdFusion developer, versus many of the other people in the community who've been doing it for 10, 15 years? I only started programming about five years ago. When I got to my first job, ColdFusion was the language they had just started using. It was a brand new development team. All of us were pretty new at it. They had picked ColdFusion. I didn't know any better. I didn't know any different, I guess I should say. I started using it. It was our own, homegrown something. I'm not even gonna call it a framework. I know that my team listening would agree with that. There was a time where I got to the point developing on it that, I just wished that we had something else, because I could look into some other communities, and see all the tooling they had, all the packages, or modules that they had to share, and see how we were feeling like we were doing everything from scratch. It's just kind of the feeling like you hear ColdFusion is dying, and I remember subscribing to that belief. What changed-*

Michaela: Well wait a minute, you didn't start it until after it had been dying for five years according to some bloggers, which is pretty ridiculous"

- Eric Peterson,
CFML and Javascript developer at O.C. Tanner in Salt Lake City, Utah

From CF Alive episode, "023 Modules Make Your Projects Have Superpowers, with Eric Peterson"

Adobe (and its predecessors) have been releasing updated versions of ColdFusion for the last 23 years, constantly adding new features and making sure that coding is faster and simpler with every new version. However, looking at a market share, it's not as popular as PHP, Java, ASP.NET, Ruby on Rails, Perl and Python.

It has gone through a lot of changes, and it has a lot of history. Some might say that's a bad thing, but I think that it is tried and trusted. It has proven to be a quality language to use for rapid application development. It has gotten to be easier and easier to use it. Everything is just a few tags away.

Let's Welcome Change

Let's welcome the increasing pace of tech change as a way to grow and specialize more. We try on this year's new "CF fashions" with excitement to see which ones fit us.

Change is life

No longer do we have fear of upgrades creating hard to find new bugs.

We overcome the negative computer press and enroll it to cheer on the new birth of modern CF.

CF Wanted: Dead or Alive

Sometimes it seems that ColdFusion is being targeted by one of those old Wild West Wanted Posters that say "Wanted, Dead or Alive, CF - Reward":

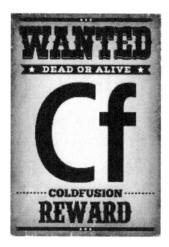

Some naysayers have said that ColdFusion was dying for the last 10 years. But it is not only still Alive; it is thriving and is now the most modern and secure web development ecosystem. Learn details on why CF is Alive in the following chapters and how you can be a part of making it even more so this year.

CF never went away. Some people might have said it was doomed but you knew in your heart that it would be triumphant in the end. This actually says a lot about the quality and experience that CF developers have developed over the years!

ColdFusion is a vibrant and modern language. I invite you to discover how in the upcoming chapters. We are proud that it is thriving and is the most state-of-the-art, reliable and secure web development ecosystem available. Bar none.

We are confidently coding easy to maintain apps in CF. Enlivened by using a tried and trusted language. Unleashing the full efficiency of using ColdFusion in our work. We inspire other developers and young programmers to explore the power of CF.

About the Author

I started programming in ColdFusion more than 20 years ago and fell in love with the power of the language. I founded a software development company called TeraTech in 1989 that specializes in ColdFusion application development, security and optimization. We have successfully delivered thousands of CF projects for organizations across the United States.

I founded the CFUnited Conference in 1999, a conference that attracted thousands of top CF developers every year. I run the annual State of the ColdFusion Union survey, which offers insights into the way CF is being used in top development shops.

In 2017 I launched the CF Alive Podcast with the goal of sharing insights from ColdFusion experts and building a stronger CF community. I have interviewed more than 60 ColdFusion experts, including Charlie Arehart, Nolan Erck, Luis Majano, Kishore Balakrishnan, as well as other top Adobe and Lucee executives who are setting the future direction of CFML.

We discuss a wide range of topics such as current practices, tools, techniques, tips and trends. The one question I ask every podcast guest is "What Would It Take to make CF more alive this year?" The answers have been fascinating - they inspired this book.

After doing all the interviews and research for this book, I became even more convinced at exactly how strong CF has become in the last few years.

Onwards!

I hope that after reading this book you will join the CF Alive revolution - become an advocate, a participant, a passionate listener of new CF Alive podcasts, a co-creator of inspiring CF blogs, a deeply committed member and potentially even become a leader that helps grow this venture far beyond you. More on that later.

Meanwhile let's deconstruct the whole CF is dying myth in in the next chapter.

CHAPTER 1

Legacy ColdFusion

Is ColdFusion dead? Not!

Let's start with a rumor that rears its head every few years: "Is ColdFusion dead?"

As someone who has been fully immersed in working with this language for more than 20 years and who is an active participant in the CF community, I can answer with a resounding absolutely not! But don't just take it from me. None of the 60 CF experts I interviewed thought it was dead either. And some of the top CF executives from Adobe had this say about actual CF sales numbers.

> *"...about seven, eight years ago when there was this kind of a feeling that ColdFusion is dying and the business was slightly on a downward trend. But over the last few years, we've seen some tremendous growth. So just to give you some numbers. So since 2012 to 2016, we've seen a 25 percent growth on the business which is roughly translates to what six to seven percent year on year."*
>
> - Tridib Roy Chowdhury, General Manager and Senior Director of Products at Adobe Systems

From CF Alive episode, "065 The Future of ColdFusion (it is Bright) with Tridib Roy Chowdhury"

And Adobe is clearly committed to ColdFusion for the foreseeable future.

"Participation in the community. ColdFusion is still alive. I don't know why that thought came that ColdFusion is dead. ColdFusion is alive and doing better and better what I've gone all a part of a lot more people who are building applications. There are still people who create some amazing applications. Until the time people asked them, "What language is that?" People always assume it to be something else. Then the moment they realize it's still ColdFusion, you should see their reaction. 'I thought ColdFusion is dead.' That's the negative attitude which people ideally like to remove from the ecosystem.

ColdFusion as a language is still doing good. There are people who are developing some amazing applications in ColdFusion. Adobe is so committed to the platform that a lot of partners open some cool applications, and solutions on top of the platform. People still are not able to get to the point that language is 23 years old and still doing good."

- Kishore Balakrishnan,
Senior Product Marketing Manager at Adobe

From CF Alive episode, "058 All about the Adobe CF Summit East 2018 ColdFusion with Kishore Balakrishnan"

When I was at Into The Box Conference I talked with some of the CF experts there, and it was interesting to hear their comments about ColdFusion. Why they are still and why they think it is the best option for web development.

"You can create so much stuff with it. It is competitive as any other language. The language itself is very versatile, and Ortus Solutions has invested so much because we believe in it..."

Jorge Reyes, Project Manager at Ortus Solutions

A very interesting story from one of the ITB attendees is by Teddie Tapawan. He stopped using the CFML at some point, but he forgot to erase this from his CV. Then he got a job offer just because of that fact! He is now 100% sure that it is coming back and is very much alive and in use. Here's the video of how he saw it.

Related Article: Developers and CIOs often ask: is ColdFusion dead?

Common legacy ColdFusion project problems

These ColdFusion project problems probably sound familiar if you have a long-term maintenance project using an older version of CF. And you're not using modern CF tools or development methods on your team.

Or if you don't notice them now, you will if one of your CF developers quits suddenly, retires or gets sick.

- You don't trust your CF app 100% (even though it is mission critical or revenue-generating)
- You have no contingency plan for a sudden developer departure or a server outage.
- Implementing new features is a painful, ad-hoc process.
- Your existing supplier provides slow or best-availability turnaround, even for simple requests.
- Every time a new freelancer works on the site, something breaks.

- Application availability (and reliability) is poor.
- You'd like to consider other options but you don't have a transition plan.

These issues can lead to other problems in your company:

- extra stress
- inefficiency
- higher cost
- reduced project velocity
- less innovation

Related Article: Easily Moving from Legacy Code Hell to Modern CFML Heaven

The issue with legacy CF versions

However many CFers are still using out of date versions from 9 years ago. In this year's State of the CF Union survey, we discovered that:

- 20% of CFers still use Adobe CF 9
- 30% still use CF 10

In case you didn't know, CF 9 went end of life on 12/31/14 and CF 10 on 5/16/17. (see Adobe Lifecycle table for the end of life dates of all versions). Between CF 9 and 10 that is a large chunk of Adobe CF users that are outside the support window. Which is a little scary because it is not just the lack of support, but also no more security hotfixes. It is like driving a car with no brakes and praying that nothing comes on the road that you need to stop for.

"A lot of people still believe that ColdFusion is like how it was ten years ago. I mean we had attended several non-ColdFusion Java conferences, we attended several Java conferences this year, and that's the knowledge that people have. So it's up to us and the community to take that knowledge forward and say, 'No, look at all the great applications we're building, look at the tooling that we have, look at the way that we can startups, and containerized applications.' And that's what's going to

make ColdFusion more alive. It will take people to start using these tools and moving forward."

- Luis Majano President of <u>Ortus Solutions</u>

From CF Alive episode, "<u>044 CommandBox + ForgeBox: ColdFusion Code, Package, Share, Go! with Luis Majano</u>"

The rise in popularity of Lucee CFML

If you can not afford to upgrade to the latest Adobe ColdFusion (ACF) then consider the free Lucee CFML. Many programmers see Lucee CFML as the open source heir to ACF. The stats from the last CF Union survey show that Lucee is more popular than ColdFusion 10 or 2016. Of course, the stats refer only to the more engaged CFers who filled out the survey. However, from discussions in the CF Slack channel and other online CF groups Lucee is gaining popularity. Especially in the cloud and for open source projects.

In case you were not aware of Lucee, it is an open source and free version of ColdFusion. It focuses on providing the same functionality as Adobe CF while using less resources and running faster. That includes faster server startup time. One of the Lucee team's core development philosophy "treats slowness as a bug".

It originally started life in 2002 as Railo, but in 2015 the project forked and the new fork was named Lucee. The Lucee Association Switzerland helps maintain and promote Lucee and some of the top CF experts in the world are members. There are also options for paid support.

"Over the last year or so CF has been going back up again, which is great. It is really a very good time to start using ColdFusion or Lucee again because lots of companies are out there that have CF applications

running. Maybe old applications, maybe new ones."
- Gert Franz, CTO Rasia Switzerland & Senior Solutions Architect at
Helsana Versicherungen AG and Lucee evangelist.

From CF Alive episode, "024 CFML Debugging Jedi Tricks and Templates, with Gert Franz"

Lucee lets you write standard CFML code using CFM and CFC files as usual. Nearly all CF tags are available and they added a bunch of new features. Developers can run old CFML apps in legacy mode. Die-hard CFers can be grateful for Lucee's progress and anticipated growth. Because it helps to dramatically enlarge the CF developer community via a free,open source version.

Lucee makes it easy for students and small projects to use the full power of ColdFusion for free. It addresses the competition from other open source languages such as PHP. Price is one factor of why CF has fallen behind some other programming languages market share. Companies that spend money on programming languages such as ACF are aware of its capabilities and benefits. The current niche of ACF lies in enterprise buyers who spend $100k+ on various other software (Oracle, MS SQL Server, SAP etc.).

How does ColdFusion stack up against its competitors?

The reason why so many developers still love/won't give up ColdFusion is that common web application tasks are easy to create in it. The built-in CFOUTPUT iterator with grouping offers fewer lines of code than PHP. Working in CF requires only 20-30% of that required by PHP.

Many developers have shared their experience of having spare time as they finished coding earlier with ColdFusion. They can then test and improve user experience, instead of typing additional lines of code in another language.

> "There are a lot of programming languages, and in the near thirty-years I've been at this, I've tried too many of them. Frankly, most of them seem like work. ColdFusion has been my great enabler, the foundation of my professional career, it's taken me around the world, to work and live among a community of fantastic colleagues and friends. Most important of all, ColdFusion has been *fun*, the thing that still makes me excited to solve all the problems."

- Grant Shepert,
UK Branch Manager at <u>Blue River Interactive Group</u>

Maintenance is easier because less code means fewer bugs to fix.

Rapid Application Development

One of the key ways that CF beats out other languages is that you can develop very rapidly in it.

> "It is a language that makes me the most productive and I can build so many applications with it in LESS time than in other languages... always coming back to CFML for rapid application development."

- Luis Majano, @ IntoTheBox Conference chat,
President of <u>Ortus Solutions</u>

Luis went on to say: "I have never understood why PHP/ASP appear to be cheaper when they use 2 to 3 times more in programming time. Small companies don't have big teams, usually up to 6 people. That leaves you with less time to take on another client. If you use ColdFusion, you can save 60-75% in time on any new project. Since it gives you time to spend on new projects even with tight budgets, your profits go up." (From the article "ColdFusion Developers and CIOs Often Ask: Is Adobe ColdFusion Dead?")

Most importantly, it keeps the pace with the recent trends in technology. With every new version released, Adobe expands the list of new features, even more than their competitors.

There isn't any better programming language for handling the development of complex applications. Some developers are calling it a "Swiss Army knife." Easy web services implementation, dozens of functions, image and PDF tools; it's a power with ease. Speed of development is the key for small and medium-sized companies. With ColdFusion, you'll get more done in less time and by putting in less effort, especially when it comes to ongoing maintenance.

The fact that the majority of US Federal government still use ColdFusion as well as Pepsico, BMW, Apple and other Fortune 500 companies, tells us a lot.

Third-party ColdFusion support

Solid third-party support for ColdFusion comes from many vendors. I detail 27 tools for CF in Chapter 2 State-of-the-Art Tools. Some popular ones include:

- FusionReactor for CF server monitoring
- Foundeo's security tools HackMyCF and FuseGuard
- Ortus Solutions suite of Box products such as the ColdBox framework, CommandBox, TestBox, MockBox and LogBox.

There are also many ColdFusion related conferences such as

- Into The Box
- MuraCon
- CFCamp
- CF Summit (East and West locations)

When we sum up all the facts we talked about, "ColdFusion is very much alive".

Despite what non-CF developers may think, there are multiple annual conferences and camps held, new versions of the language constantly introduced, and it still used by 75% of the Fortune 100 companies and the US government.

CF offers an excellent ROI with increased developer productivity for medium to large-scale companies. Rapid development in ColdFusion increases developer output by 30%, and that percentage goes up when you use the modern CF methods and tools in this book. Your staff will not spend more time than it has to on clearing bugs and maintaining complex functionality.

My considered assessment is that CF is more alive right now than before. And with your and other CF community members active support, it will become more vibrant in the future.

Summary

- CF is alive and growing
- CF beats the competitor for ease of use and rapid development
- Legacy CF can be modernized by upgrading your CF server, development methods and tools

Let's look at the Modernizing CF in detail in the next chapter.

CHAPTER 2

Modernization

"Software innovation, like almost every other kind of innovation, requires the ability to collaborate and share ideas with other people, and to sit down and talk with customers and get their feedback and understand their needs."

-Bill Gates, co-founder Microsoft

Software development is always evolving. And fast! In fact, they change at such a rapid pace that the next big thing is always around the corner. Keeping up can be difficult for some developers and organizations. That doesn't mean we shouldn't do our best to keep up. Should we reject this or embrace it? Change is inevitable so let's make the most of it. By modernizing the way we work with ColdFusion, we can help CF become much more alive.

"ColdFusion has given me career-wise something more than any other tool, and that's success. I've been able to help customers win. We build sites, they do what they need, we're able to keep timelines. It is not a 100% win all around, but I've looked at our success ratio, and the ratio of competitors, and when I'm getting faster delivery and a higher success ratio, then it's what I call modern ColdFusion."

- John Farrar, CEO, SOSensible Group

From CF Alive episode, "018 VUE More With Less, with John Farrar"

Related: Which is better for your Company and ColdFusion Apps? Control or Speed?

Use Modern Technologies

To make ColdFusion modern you need to use modern methods and tools with it. A lot of the buzz about younger languages is to do with the way they are used and the tools employed. This chapter gives 27 modern tools and frameworks that you can use on your projects. They will help you speed up development and improve code quality.

Using modern CF also makes it easier to attract quality CF developers to your company. And helps bring younger blood into the CF Community.

> *"I'm proud to use ColdFusion because it makes me productive. It is a great language. It solves my problems and it solves them more quickly and easily than some of the languages so that's why I'm proud to use ColdFusion is because how productive it makes me and the modern language that it's become."*
>
> - Brad Wood,
> Software Architect and Platform Evangelist Ortus Solutions

From CF Alive episode, "029 Design Patterns for amazing app architecture (16 patterns), with Brad Wood"

Use the Current Version

"...CF is also very forgiving in that way for migrations. I do a lot of migration, so very few problems going from 10 to 11 to 16. You really learn to appreciate working with ColdFusion."

-Mike Collins, Senior ColdFusion consultant at <u>SupportObjective</u>

From CF Alive episode, "<u>062 Scaling Your ColdFusion Applications (Clusters, Containers and Load Tips) with Mike Collins</u>"

New software versions are released for a reason. They provide new updated technologies and features to enhance your CF experience. New versions often fix major security and performance issues too. So what version are the CFers currently using? According to the <u>State of the CF Union 2018</u>, the 4 year old ColdFusion 11 is still the most popular. There are still CFers using the 9 year old CF 9. It's time for an update. If you are using a version older than CF 11, there is a very good reason to update now. Adobe has declared these versions at end of life. This means there will be no more hotfixes and security updates. If you cannot afford a new ACF license, then consider the free open source Lucee 5 for your CFML needs.

"It's because it solves every problem which is thrown at me which is true. I think that the most important thing is super flexible, and I can do anything I want with it. Of course there are cases where other technologies, or other solutions are more appropriate. But that it got me started. Started my career, and I've been able to do everything I needed to do until now with it. I always keep an eye out on what else is there. But I haven't really run into anything which is that easy to me to use. So haven't switched. I still love CF, and I'm not walking away from it."

- Guust Nieuwenhuis, Managing Partner &
Full Stack Web Wizard at <u>Orange Lark</u>

From CF Alive episode, "048 CF Continuous Integration Plumbing with Bitbucket Pipelines with Guust Nieuwenhuis"

Many ColdFusion developers and users do not upgrade to newer versions because of the fear of change. Perhaps they don't know all the benefits of the updates or want to stay in their comfort zone. One way to calm your nerves about switching versions is to go to conferences. Conferences provide a great backbone of knowledge to any new and upcoming CF version. Talking with fellow CFers who have been through the same upgrade you are considering can address your concerns.

> *"CFML has become a completely modern language. I'm proud to use CF because it is a great language. It has its quirks but hey, show me a language that doesn't."*
>
> - Mark Drew, Director at CMD

From CF Alive episode, "035 Getting started fast with Docker, with Mark Drew"

If you can't make it to a CF conference then the CFML slack channel is a free and location independent way to share questions and experiences. Another great place to catch all the new information is the CF Alive podcast. Here up-to-date topics are discussed with ColdFusion experts on the cutting edge. Using current versions is a great way to help keep CF alive as well. By updating, it shows that you have faith in your platform. It means you are ready to continue using ColdFusion. If we stop updating our ColdFusion, we will see it die.

"It's been the language I've used 100% of the time in the last 18 years of my professional life. I love working in ColdFusion, it is both comfortable to work in yet also stretches me as I continually find new things I can do with it in every release. There's been a lot of effort over the years to evolve ColdFusion and keep pace with other languages and modern programming concepts."

- <u>Ed Bartram</u>, Senior Web Developer at Senior Market Sales

From CF Alive episode, "<u>080 Assert Control Over Your Legacy Applications (TestBox Quick Start) with Ed Bartram</u>"

Related article: <u>Comprehensive list of ColdFusion Conferences 2017, and What Can We expect in 2018</u>

Adapt and Integrate

"Nowadays, there are so many languages, and so many technologies. It's great to learn other technologies, and learn other languages. It is important that we have to be all around developers not only as single language kind of developer. So that is really important nowadays, but I always come back to CFML. I love its power. It integrates as a middleware for all kinds of technologies."

- Luis Majano President of <u>Ortus Solutions</u>

From CF Alive episode, "<u>044 CommandBox + ForgeBox: ColdFusion Code, Package, Share, Go! with Luis Majano</u>"

Another thing that would help make CF more alive is integrating new technologies. There is a lot of new CF related tech out there. Using it can help draw in younger programmers and invigorate older ones. And make your organization's apps more reliable, efficient and secure too. For example, CF support guru Mike Collins uses the <u>Vue.js Progressive JavaScript Framework</u> in his ColdFusion apps. He says he has been seeing some of the freshest new content coming from there. It would be great if ColdFusion is able to integrate more fully with Vue.js. Bring more vibrance to CF and incorporate other technologies.

> *"I just always had a passion for ColdFusion and I just you know it was described to me one time as kind of the Swiss Army knife of application tools and it always seems like there's a way to do anything with ColdFusion. No matter what the problem is there's always a way to solve it. You integrate whether even if you have to do some Java package or something, there's always a way to integrate it into ColdFusion. And lots of great resources out there that are from all the experts on the Internet."*
>
> - Mike Collins, Senior ColdFusion consultant at <u>SupportObjective</u>

From CF Alive episode, "<u>062 Scaling Your ColdFusion Applications (Clusters, Containers and Load Tips) with Mike Collins</u>"

Related Podcast: <u>VUE More With Less, with John Farrar</u>

Invest in CF

As I mentioned at the beginning of this chapter, organizations and development teams need to evolve. Many are still using outdated versions of ColdFusion, old development methods and are missing out on the latest tools.

"We are proud to use it because any engineer is proud to use best of breed tools. And CFML has always been in our opinion a best of breed tools for what it does, for web applications and other kinds of things you can build in CFML. So, we certainly believe that. We use it, we continue to be proud to use it because like any craftsman, we like to use the best possible tools."

- Patrick Quinn, CoFounder, CEO and CTO of Webapper

From CF Alive episode, "039 CFML Secrets with Patrick Quinn (AWS, Lucee and SeeFusion)"

Some even use only CF tags in their code and nothing else. No CF Script. No CFCs or Object-Oriented programming.

Some of the reasons for not writing Modern ColdFusion include:

- Fear of Learning New Things
- Belief that New Tech is Overly Complicated
- Too Many Files
- Too much Code to maintain
- Fear of Inadequate Problem Solving
- Unaware of New Tech
- Unable to Budget Time and Money for learning.

This does not bode well for the future of ColdFusion currently existing at corporations. Some are still talking about writing code as if it were 2001. Let's help them fix that problem. With the use of new technologies, it is very easy to convert your legacy code to modern CFML.

"...nobody is going to come work for procedural programming. I mean nobody. No wonder nobody wants to go do ColdFusion because they don't want to be working with procedural code. So if corporations don't do this, ColdFusion will not be alive anymore. So the corporations really need to modernize. That's the first thing."

- Luis Majano, President of Ortus Solutions

From CF Alive episode, "012 Extreme Testing and Slaying the Dragons of ORM with Luis Majano"

Security

Security concerns are an important part of any programming language. No platform is 100% secure. But there are many tools and best practices out there to help you be as secure as you can be. Keeping a tight grip on security measures is pivotal to keeping CF alive. Nobody wants to use a very insecure development platform.

Auto Lockdown

With the release of ColdFusion 2018 came a new wave of security improvements. The new auto lockdown feature is one of them. This is a great new feature for those with security concerns. The days of having to manually lock down your server are in the past. With the new auto lockdown feature, you can implement lockdown of your production server with one simple click. Full lockdown procedures will be systemically applied making sure all security measures are fail-safe and within compliance. After the lockdown, all systems are continuously monitored for breaches and potential security threats.

Official Lockdown Guides

For those who prefer to lockdown their CF server manually there are the still the official ColdFusion Lockdown guides. A lot of CF developers don't even know they exist. Or do but don't use them in detail. They were written with the help of CF Security Guru Pete Freitag. The lockdown guides are free PDF downloads that show step by step procedures on locking down your server for tight security. Complete with screenshots. They cover everything including Apache and IIS. If everybody were to follow the guide, most ColdFusion hacks would not happen in the first place.

Security Code Analyzer

Adobe also released a new Security Code Analyzer. This is another top-of-the-line security update from Adobe. Every CF expert knows the weight that a great security system can carry. This tool pushes levels of security to a new level. It automatically scans and searches your application code for any existing security vulnerabilities and any potential security breaches. It determines the exact vulnerable code, type of vulnerability, and severity level. After all of that, the analyzer presents you with the option of removing and repairing the problem via recommended means. This may be the security tool that we have all been waiting on.

Maintain Consistent Server Architecture

This may seem like a no-brainer, but you would be surprised how many do not follow this simple best practice. You should maintain consistency throughout the development, testing, and live phases of your project. If you don't have consistent development, testing, and production environments, you will constantly be fighting an uphill battle. A systemized workflow decreases your cost of time and money. It also increases your security and application performance.

Related: 11 Best Practices for a new Adobe ColdFusion Project

Clean up unused deadwood code

Unused old code and even whole directories of "deadwood" not only create maintenance confusion, they are a security risk. Often older code is less securely written. Or might be a test version that comments out login checks. In my experience hackers often penetrate a CF server via deadwood code.

The solution? Take the time to clean it up. And even better use a modern development workflow with Git that does not even copy test code to your production server.

Use CF Security Tools

You can increase CF server security even more by using CF security expert Pete Freitag's tools HackMyCF and FuseGuard. See Chapter 2 State-of-the-art Tools section on Security Tools for details.

Reliability

What does it mean to have a reliable CF server? Reliability refers to the server's ability to perform consistently according to specifications. Reliability is extremely important for ColdFusion. It can be accomplished through many ways.

- Defensive coding, checking parameters against allowed ranges or values helps bugs from spreading between modules.
- Using good CF error handling stops errors from totally destroying your user's experience.
- Over-engineering servers with more RAM, CPU than the minimum you need.
- If you host with an ISP then use a dedicated or cloud hosting option rather than shared.
- Clustering several servers using a load balancer, so if one goes down due to a crash or applying updates the other servers in the cluster keep your app live. You can cluster both CF server and database servers.

- Hot backup of code and data
- Regularly applying updates and hotfixes
- Testing new code and updates on a staging server before deploying to production
- Separating different apps or even parts of the same app between different instances of CF (on ColdFusion Enterprise) or on different servers increases reliability. If one app or part of an app crashes it doesn't affect the others.
- Containerizing your CF apps using Docker in the Cloud with auto scaling and auto failover adds to reliability.

A reliable server can make sure that your CF application runs the way it is supposed to. 24/7. By maintaining reliable CF servers, CF can be more alive by building trust amongst users and fellow ColdFusion developers.

"We've got some massive applications that are being built, that are driving business and really critical business for heavy hitting companies, right. And I think that's where I'm proud to be a part of this whole initiative and I think that ColdFusion is certainly not dead and it's growing for us. And it is a technology that I think people need to try it before they go ahead and put it down."

- Elishia Dvorak, Technical Marketing Manager at <u>Adobe</u>

From CF Alive episode, "<u>030 Everything CF Summit That You Need to Know, with Elishia Dvorak</u>"

Scalability

Scalability means your CF app and server infrastructure can easily handle extra load. Scalability is extremely important for mission critical CF projects. You want your CF apps to be able to handle any amount of traffic that they come across without slowdowns or even worse server crashes. Scalable applications keep ColdFusion alive by providing you and and your clients with reliable performance. Without scalability, your CF app would be useless under peak load.

Many of the reliability tips above help with scaling.

Writing code and designing your database for scaling is also key. As is CF and JVM configuration. All CF servers need tuning to scale well.

To find out if your CF app and servers scale before they get hit with real load, I recommend that you load test them with simulated traffic. There are many load testing software tools that you can use. From the free Apache JMeter to thousands of dollars for Micro Focus (formerly HP and Mercury) LoadRunner.

You also want to simulate a realistic amount of test data. SQL statements that run fast with a hundred test rows of data may run slow as a snail when millions of rows are there. This also include coding a data archiving policy to move old data into backups.

With traditional dedicated CF servers you also need to do capacity planning. Figuring out ahead of time how many servers you need for different load levels. So that you can buy and set them up weeks before they are needed. Fortunately, there is a another free tool that you can use to make your servers auto scaling. Docker.

Containerize

So what is Docker? It runs your applications in virtual containers. It modernizes your legacy development and deployment processes. It makes your apps more reliable and scalable. Because when there is extra load, a new server instance can be automatically spun up in seconds. And if a server in your Docker cluster crashes, it too can respun up in seconds.

Docker has been around since 2010, but it has grown in the CF world in the last few years thanks to CF server images for it and the CommandBox tool for installing them in containers in seconds. (More details on CommandBox in the next chapter)

Containerization can do great things for you and your CF team:

- Speed up the App Building Process for New Developers
- Integrate Modern Methodologies and Automate Development Pipelines
- Infinitely Scale your Apps in the Cloud
- Provide an Integrated Security Framework

Building modern apps is a crucial process for the future. They allow your apps to be run across a complex-hybrid cloud environment. This allows for better DevOps, and builds CI/CD (Continuous Integration/Continuous Deployment) apps more easily. Along with these benefits, you can take advantage of new innovations such as architecting your app using microservices.

Docker vs Vagrant

Some CFers use Vagrant for virtualized machines. But, there are huge advantages of Docker over Vagrant.

DOCKER	VAGRANT
Containerization	Virtualization
Low Overhead--Fast Boot Up	High Overhead--Slow Boot Up
Relies on Security of Container-easier to secure	Relies on Security of VM- more difficult to secure
Containers are launched directly from kernel space.	VM's must be launched on the existing host's OS

If you are managing multiple VM's, then maybe Vagrant is for you. But for most CFers, making the switch to Docker is the logical choice. Docker Containers can manage your apps much more efficiently and save resources while doing so.

Why use CF in the Cloud?

Docker makes it easy to run CF in the Cloud. So why is using a CF in the cloud great?

- Lets you get your applications up and running with minimal upfront cost of new dedicated servers.
- Allows for great immediate scalability of your application.
- Improves operational efficiency, productivity, and agility

These can all be accomplished through using Docker with any cloud provider such as <u>AWS</u>, <u>Azure</u>, <u>Google Cloud</u>, <u>Digital Ocean</u>.

Adobe and Docker

While Ortus CommandBox has provided unofficial CF images for Docker for several years, the <u>official Adobe Docker image for CF 2018</u> just came out. However, Adobe fell short on cloud pricing because it still uses perpetual pricing on most cloud providers (ie you pay by the server). So if you need ten extra CF containers for 3 hours during the SuperBowl ad that your company displays, you need to pay for ten extra ACF licences - rather than the more common cloud pricing model of paying by the hour of use. This gives the free open-source Lucee a tremendous advantage for auto scaling. The only form of cloud pricing available for ColdFusion currently is via AWS (Amazon Web Services) Marketplace. This is pricing in which you pay by the hour. Adobe could help keep CF more alive by teaming up with Docker and providing cloud pricing on all cloud providers.

Deployment

One big issue CF developers have is choosing their form of deployment. The most popular option is for In-House hosting. But the trend is to outsource hosting to an ISP or the Cloud. Here are the options:

- Shared Hosting
- Managed Servers

- Dedicated Machines
- Cloud hosting

To put this in a metaphor, shared hosting is like a hostel dormitory. You share a room with all the other people. If someone gets drunk and throws up on the bunk bed, you have a problem. A managed server is like an apartment complex where there are other apartments but they are walled off from each other. A dedicated machine is like having a detached house - you have to furnish it and fix the faucet when it leaks. Still some work, but you don't have to worry about your bed being vomited on. Cloud hosting is like having a virtual dedicated house - one that you can instantly clone for more space when a horde of out of town guests arrive.

Flexible Container Cloud Hosting

As mentioned earlier, the number one solution for software deployment is containerization using Docker. There are several orchestration layer tools that you can use to make it even more powerful:

- Kubernetes
- Heroku
- Dokku

A Docker orchestration layers lets you configure your application load between containers. If it reaches a certain threshold, then orchestration can automatically deploy another CF server with your app code "pre-installed" in the image. There is automatic load balancing between all containers running your app. This gives an unheard of level of flexibility.

Modern Testing Environment

Using a modern testing environment is critical to keeping CF alive. The lack of a mature testing environment can lead to absolute chaos during the run-up to deploying new code. Minimize the amount of resources you will spend going back to revise broken code. This also prevents established bugs from spreading by detecting them early. There are many quality improvements that are made through using modern testing such as:

- Code Coverage
- Automated Testing
- Code Review
- Bug Modeling and Prevention

Use portable testing environments -- such as CF Builder-- as well. The benefit to using portable environments is making the reuse of the development environment configuration much easier.

A typical set up includes:

- A staging server where you test (ideally using Docker to mirror your production setup)
- A Continuous Integration tool such as Jenkins that automatically pushes new changes for testing
- Automated testing using TestBox
- Automatic reporting of any bugs and preventing buggy branches being merged into production code

Poor Testing and Deployment

Poor testing and deployment can trip up and injure a project on the last lap of the race.

Bugs in Production

Too many bugs are showing up in production. One bug in production is one bug too many. However, there are systems in which bugs are popping up every day in production. Use a modern testing environment to prevent this. See the Modern Testing Environment section below for more details on this.

Realistic Data Load

Another common problem is that the application works fine when it has only a few hundred records in the database. The problem arises when millions of rows are in the database after running live for a while. The application no longer works well, and pages can take minutes to load. The server might crash too under such a heavy load. Load test your applications prior to deployment!

Common Database Problems

According to a poll of CF developers, half of them have database issues. Often database issues are behind a lot of these deployment issues. Either the database wasn't planned out well to start with or wasn't tested with correct data volumes. Common issues include:

- Slow Queries
- Complex SQL
- Poor Error Handling
- Security Issues

Solutions for Poor Testing and Deployment

Here are some of the potential solutions for poor testing and deployment.

Formal Acceptance Testing

Have a formal acceptance-testing period for 2-4 weeks. Where your end users test your app against the written requirements documents. Allow beta testers to determine what part of your app and code are correct. This helps to locate bugs and UI problem areas within the project before going live.

Code Review

Have another developer review your code. And you review their code. This is sometimes called peer code review. It is actually much quicker at finding bugs and poor quality code than testing. A side benefit is that several team members understand the whole code base and so can make maintenance changes if a key developer is out of the office.

Staging Server

It's surprising how many ColdFusion developers don't have a staging server in addition to their production server. This is a server where you do testing. You can verify everything is working properly with your app before pushing it into production. Additionally, you may do load testing on this staging server. The staging server should be an accurate mirror of the production server in terms of hardware and software. This way any issues with the environment will show up before you go live. Docker makes mirroring your production server to staging very easy.

Automated Deployment Scripts

Automate your deployment by using scripts. These are particularly useful when you have a clustered environment. Scripts automatically copy new code out of Git. Then, they deploy the code out to all the different servers in the cluster. Take the same approach with any database changes. Deploy those across your cluster of database servers using a deployment script. Using automated deployment scripts can prevent a whole class of bugs with missing files from happening in the first place.

More about script tools in the Continuous Integration section below.

Load Testing

As mentioned in the Scalability section, load testing is key to having an app that you know ahead of time can handle expected traffic volumes. Make sure your server is tuned correctly for the volume of data and users you expect. Run realistic load tests on the app. This is crucial for a successful deployment. Load testing software simulates users entering data and clicking on your pages. Some software even allows for random data and supplying user/passwords to log in to a secure section of your app. They can also simulate the delays between clicks caused by human "thinking time".

In addition to testing expected load, do destructive testing. Find out at what load your code and server will crash. This lets you identify bottlenecks in the system. Use this as part of your capacity planning, to predict when you will need to buy extra memory, CPUs, or servers.

Related Podcast: Scaling Your ColdFusion Applications (Clusters, Containers and Load Tips) with Mike Collins

Deployment Issue Summary

A successful deployment is one that is stress free and goes smoothly. Everything should work fine. An unsuccessful deployment has constant bugs or the app is crashing. This is made even worse when different versions of code overwrite each other. The top two issues of CFers in relation to testing and deployment are:

- Too Many Bugs
- No Formal Testing

Be sure to properly test your app to catch the bugs before they get to production.

Continuous Integration (CI) Deployment Tools

According to the 2018 State of the CF Union, 44% of CFers polled do not automate or use CI deployment tools. If you are not automating your builds, you are missing out on saving time and improving your deployment and testing process. Because at the click of a button you can update your staging or production code directly from your source code repository. Never again will you forget to update all the files on your server. Plus if you spin up a new server it can be automatically set up exactly the same way as your other servers.

For those who do CI, Jenkins is the most popular program.

Other options include:

- GitLab
- Bamboo
- Ant
- Grunt
- Travis

- Gulp
- Bitbucket Pipelines

Change Tracking

A great way to make CF more alive for your project is to use a change tracking management system. Why do so though? If you just fix bugs as they are reported without tracking, it is easy to forget to fix some of them. Or prioritize the ones you do fix. You also can have a hard time figuring out who on your team fixed which bug a few weeks later when it causes an unexpected problem. Small changes can soon add up to a large amount of extra effort and time.

Popular change trackers among CFers include:

- JIRA
- Bugzilla
- Trac
- FogBugz
- GitHub

A new kid on the block of bug trackers is The Bug Squasher . I interviewed the founder Kirk Deis about bug tracking in general and his tool in this episode Better Bug Squashing (New Issue Tracking Tool) with Kirk Deis

What You Get With a Great Issue Tracking System

- Different access levels for clients, testers, developers and managers
- New issues can be classified as bug reports
- Change requests available that include the date/time reported, who reported it, severity description of the issue, details on how to reproduce it, and screenshot upload
- Create a unique ID to reference the issue
- Assign issues to developers
- Auto status change of an issue between new, fixed, tested, out of scope.

- Workflow can automatically email the issue submitter and assigned developer on a status change
- Allow comments on the issue as the status changes
- Keep a history of edits to the issue
- Report on all open and closed issues by status, severity etc. Graphs of number of issues per week

Change Process

In addition to the change tracking system, you need to have a process for determining what changes are in scope and out of scope. Here is one way:

- Track all bug reports and change requests in one system.
- Review them against the system requirements. This can tell you what is and what is not in scope.
- Have two separate people review scope and change code. One to review scope. One to change code. Often the Project Manager will do the first role and the CF developer the second.

If a change is out of scope, how do you communicate that with the client? Many issue tracking systems automatically email clients when an issue is reported. This allows people to view the status of all issues online. However, regular status meetings between you and your client are highly recommended to prevent misunderstandings.

Related: 11 Best Practices for a new Adobe ColdFusion Project

Client Education on the Change Process

Whatever system you use, I recommend you educate your client up front about your change process. Let them know that only issues reported in it will be considered for fixing. It is easy for clients under stress to bypass a system. They have a tendency to contact developers directly with their concerns. You need to enforce the use of the system to get the benefits of a tracking system. Require developers to either say that a change must go through the system. Or better yet, tell them to talk to the project manager about any changes. Often developers want to please the client and are not assertive. Providing support for them to politely say "No" helps here.

Improve CFML

The best way to hit home that ColdFusion is still alive is to improve CFML itself. This shows that the creators of and community still believe in CF. There are a number of ways that this can be accomplished:

- Learn from other languages
- Better 3rd party tool support
- Better integration and sample CF code in other products/SaaS

"Because in the last 22 years I haven't found anything better. Bearing in mind, at any point in time, I usually have five or six clients, most of them are still ColdFusion, some of them are Java, but like I said, I worked on PHP and I worked on .Net. Those things don't have anything better than ColdFusion as for what it's doing, which is providing, the best of what it does is to provide a server mechanism to power front ends, whether your browsers or phones or devices or whatever. None of those other tools are any better. The reality is, there's a lot of fashion in development, and things go out of fashion.

What we must never forget, in my opinion, is without ColdFusion, the web as we've come to know it, the dynamic web would have been a long time coming. We have to remember, ColdFusion was around before Bill Gates thought the internet was anything worth thinking about, or at least the web."

-<u>Mike Brunt</u>, Senior Server Engineer at Go2RIA

From CF Alive episode, "009 Tuning & Troubleshooting ColdFusion Using Native Tools with Mike Brunt"

Influence from Other Languages

A great way to broaden CFML is to take ideas from other programming languages and their development tools. This way we can keep CF up with the state-of-the-art of software development. Some major languages to check out include:

- Java
- Ruby
- Python
- PHP
- C++
- Node/JavaScript

"What in particular I enjoy about coding in CFML, is the power and flexibility of the meta programming which we use day to day. You're not stuck with what the language gives you. You can really nice, and easily, use meta programming to extend it to create your own frameworks, and I know other languages do that, but it's always much more direct to do things in CFML without ... Compare it to Ruby that does some nice syntactic sugar around that. It's more straight forward. It's not quite so obscure as a language. It reads much better."

- Dominic Watson, Technical Director at Pixl8 Interactive

From CF Alive episode, "007 Marketing Automation using the Preside Platform with Dominic Watson"

Some of the 3rd party tools for CF are already taking ideas from other languages and their tools. For example CommandBox implements some ideas from Linux package managers.

"I can be super-productive and I can talk to other languages and be a polyglot programmer because I don't have to spend tons of time. When it comes to fun stuff like spreadsheets, or PDF generation, dealing with horrible external libraries, I can just make it happen within CF in a couple of lines of code. I love that."

-Brian Klaas, Senior Technology Officer at the Johns Hopkins Bloomberg School of Public Health's Center for Teaching and Learning

From CF Alive episode, "037 Level Up Your ColdFusion Web Apps With Amazon Web Services, with Brian Klaas"

Better Tooling Support

From a developer standpoint, better tooling support is needed for CFML. There are plenty of great tools out there (which I discuss at length in Chapter 2 Tools). However, native CFML needs to be improved to give more support to them. We have seen official Docker images from Lucee and more recently CF 2018. And support added for distributed databases. More support for other tools will definitely make CF more alive.

This can be achieved through direct collaboration with third party tool providers. Work together with those who make the platform better and easier to use. This action would build rapport with the companies and inspire them to produce other great products. Also, it could motivate new companies to pay more attention to CFML.

A large percentage of CFers still use Adobe Dreamweaver. Yet, support for CFML was removed in the last few years. Thankfully, it can be put back directly by CFers. Adobe should reintroduce updated direct CFML support for Dreamweaver. It would only make sense for Adobe products to support each other. At least as an advanced installation option if you don't want other Dreamweaver users to get confused.

> *"I've been using it since '98 and it's always got the job done for me. I've found it to be a very productive language. It's a language that has gotten better over the years. The scripting support I'm enjoying using full script CFCs these days. I'm enjoying using these things. I still find it productive."*

- Pete Freitag, President at <u>Foundeo, Inc</u>

From CF Alive episode, "<u>020 Secrets of High-Security ColdFusion Code, With Pete Freitag</u>"

Integration

The most used programming language is Java. There are many nodes of integration between CFML and Java. Could it be more tightly coupled? What about other languages?

> *"CF has been the right tool at many of my programming instances to cater to the right solution, build a community and of course friends. My company, MitrahSoft, is a CF focused company and we love the Rapid Application Development approach with CF which complements very well with the spirited Agile Development approach."*

- Saravanamuthu J, Founder & CTO at <u>MitrahSoft</u>

Then there are third party libraries and SaaS products. Some come with CFML example code already but many do not. Brad Wood has been leading the crusade to get CF listed in example code by both providing sample CFML code and organizing other CFers to email the companies requesting CF example code. But there are many more to do and help from other CFers in this area would improve things a lot.

Seeing CF listed along with Java, Ruby and Python on third party library websites helps counter the idea that CF is dead among other developers.

> *"One of the reasons why I'm proud to use CF is because it makes me a more productive developer. When I want to go outside of CF, it's really easy for me to have CF talk to something else, regardless of what it is. For us right now, it's a lot of Node apps, Node services. CF talks HTTP. HTTP is the lingua franca of the web. It's lingua franca of Amazon Web Services. In Amazon Web Services, everything you do is HTTP request, even when you use the AWS SDK for Java. It's making HTTP requests in the background, and ColdFusion's part of that."*
>
> - Brian Klaas, Senior Technology Officer at the Johns Hopkins Bloomberg School of Public Health's Center for Teaching and Learning

From CF Alive episode, "037 Level Up Your ColdFusion Web Apps With Amazon Web Services, with Brian Klaas"

Lucee CFML

Lucee is the open-source version of CFML. It is popular among the CF community due to its ease of use and it being free. According to the 2018 State of the CF Union, 40% of CFers use Lucee 5. That is an astounding number. Improving Lucee would definitely keep CF alive.

> *"We're also a member of the Lucee Association, so I'm really proud to be involved with that and to help open source software stay alive and, perhaps, one day, that side of CFML will be what keeps CFML alive.*

That's what I hope. I hope Adobe ColdFusion never does drop it and that it remains strong and all of those things, but for us, we're really proud to be a part of that and to contribute to that to make sure it doesn't die."
- Dominic Watson, Technical Director at Pixl8 Interactive

From CF Alive episode, "007 Marketing Automation using the Preside Platform with Dominic Watson"

Lucee contains everything you need as a developer to get started with ColdFusion and do much of what Adobe ColdFusion does. It runs most ACF code without change.

Lucee uses the same tag-based language as ColdFusion as well as a full set of script based features, therefore making programming easy. Using Lucee, promotes using CFML thus, promoting the use of Adobe ColdFusion as well.

Because it is free, Lucee tends to be where new CFML users tend to start. So supporting Lucee is a great way to help keep ColdFusion alive.

"More support of Lucee. I think there's a very strong argument to be made that the most exciting things that are coming out of the CFML world are happening with Lucee. The pace of developments, the implementing of best practices, and from the broader software world. More of this is happening with Lucee. Of course, Lucee is more friendly to cloud environments just because of the fact that it's an open source software product."
- Patrick Quinn, CoFounder, CEO and CTO of Webapper

From CF Alive episode, "039 CFML Secrets with Patrick Quinn (AWS, Lucee and SeeFusion)"

Free version of Adobe ColdFusion?

Some new users to CFML may be driven away by the cost of the platform (currently $2499 for Standard and $9499 for Enterprise edition). And perhaps they don't feel that they would use all the features in CF 2018. Of course the developer edition is free and you can host your CF apps at ISPs for low monthly fees.

One thing Adobe could do to keep up with Lucee and eliminate these problems is to promote their own free version. Call it CF Lite. This would have the basic necessities to use CFML. This could encourage beginner developers to use CF. After outgrowing CF Lite, users could be more motivated to swap over to the Standard or Enterprise editions.

It could also be given away as part of Adobe's current education outreach program. Graduating developers would already be comfortable with the basics of CFML. This would make the transition into full Adobe ColdFusion that much easier. And this could help to combat Adobe's losses to Lucee.

More Open Source CF Modules

More open source CF projects help other CFers develop apps faster. When you can plug in an existing tested module rather than coding it yourself, you save time and bugs. One of the best places to find open-source CF code is ForgeBox. ForgeBox has hundreds of modules for CF already and is growing. If Adobe were to show support to ForgeBox, CFlib and other CF code repositories, that would encourage more CFers to create new packages to share. That would help make CF more alive.

Summary

- Upgrade your CF server to the latest version.
- Write secure code and use CF security tools to protect your server.
- Containerize your apps with Docker for more reliable and scalable apps.
- Use proper deployment strategies and Continuous Integration tools.
- Use a modern testing environment and tools.
- Use a Change tracking management system.
- Improve CFML with ideas from other languages.
- Try out the Lucee open source CFML.
- Contribute open source CF modules to ForgeBox.

Let's dig deeper into modern CF tools in the next chapter.

CHAPTER 3

State-of-the-Art Tools

"Lead roles are fun, but I'm especially happy other more colorful, supporting stuff has come along."

-Paul Giamatti, American Actor and Producer

If CFML programming were a play, Adobe ColdFusion would be the leading role. Lucee CFML is a costar. What about the supporting cast? There are many state-of-the-art tools that fill those positions. These tools are pivotal to making ColdFusion modern and alive. From containerization, source control, package management, frameworks, IDEs, testing and deployment. By further integration of third-party tools, we can watch ColdFusion develop into a rising star in the world of web development.

> *"There is a lot of modernity and vibrancy to the work being done in CF today, but you have to know where to look: it's in Docker, Lucee, CommandBox, hierarchical MVC, and easier-than-ever cloud deployment. It's very much a community-driven enterprise and anybody who wants to see the best practices should be on CFML Slack, talking to the people who are doing them!"*
>
> -Samuel Knowlton, Founder of inLeague

From CF Alive episode, "061 The Great ColdFusion Entrepreneurial Adventure (from side jobs to freelancing to your own biz) with Samuel Knowlton"

Containerization Tools

As I explained in the prior chapter, containerization is one of several key new state-of-the-art development techniques. Jumping on board now would help keep CF alive and become more modern. Using it will allow for maximum reliability, scalability and portability for your applications. It can also save you a considerable amount of resources.

Containerization makes apps much more portable by allowing these apps to run on any machine without requiring their own VM. Along with portability, containerization is much less resource intensive. Think of the resource comparison between an entire VM and smaller kernels. By sharing kernels, you can easily place more applications on a single server. Containerized apps also launch much faster than VM-based apps. Containerized apps may launch in less than one second compared to the several minutes required to start of VMs. Fortunately for us, there are several tools that help ColdFusion with containerization.

- Docker
  - Docker is driving the modern container movement. It is the only program (as of now) to be able to manage every app across the hybrid cloud. The first step to using Docker is to modernize your legacy apps. Docker's MTA kit does this automatically without changing a single line of code. Docker also packages your apps into isolated containers making them portable to any infrastructure. This eliminates the "won't work on my machine" problem. Docker also enables the use of microservice application development due to its lightweight containers.
- Portainer.io
  - Portainer is an open source Docker management UI. It is specifically designed for use with Docker. It has the latest

support for Docker, Docker Swarm, and Swarm nodes. It is an easy program to use, deploying with only one Docker command.

- CommandBox Images and Containers
  - o CommandBox has developed Docker container images for Adobe ColdFusion or Lucee CFML from ACF 9 and up and Lucee 4 and up. According to Ortus CEO Luis Majano, there's no excuse for people not to be leveraging containers with ColdFusion these days.

Source Control Tools

Nolan Erck has the best explanation for source control. He says that source control is like the librarian for your source code. A library keeps track of what books have been checked out and by whom. Source control tools do the same thing for all your CF code and config files. Using source control is a best practice in the industry. Using it can make CF more alive by giving you a strong security for your code.

A Source control tool lets you create and maintain an archive of what source code has been created, changed or edited and by who and when. In the event of your laptop or server crashing, it allows you to retrieve your original source code was before the crash. It also lets you get your code back if you edit it by mistake - or if a teammate does.

You can use source code control on any files in your CF project, such as:
- ColdFusion Source Code
- Docker Containers Config
- Images
- Plain Text Documentation

The best source control tool is the open source Git. Git is a distributed version control system that handles everything for all size projects with maximum speed and efficiency. Git is very easy to learn and features cheap local branching, convenient staging areas, and multiple workflows.

Benefits of Using Git

- Git allows branches to be created to test code with. Once the branch has been properly tested it may be moved into the main code.
- Git allows all changes to be saved. Reverting back to a previous version has never been easier.
- Git allows you to compare changed files among versions.

There are other Git tools that can be used with ColdFusion as well.

- GitHub
  - GitHub offers all the source control and version control features of Git. It even has its own added features such as social networking functions.
- Tower
  - Tower is a Git client designed to help you master the source control of Git. With Tower, you are able to access all of the functions of Git easily with its own array of performance boosting processes.
- BitBucket
  - BitBucket offers support for distributed version control to allow easy collaboration of code for your team. It gives teams a one stop shop to plan projects, code, test and deploy. A key benefit to using BitBucket over Git is the privacy that you will receive.
- TortoiseGit
  - TortoiseGit is a Windows shell interface to Git. It is fully open-sourced and can be rebuilt with free software if you want to customize it. Main interactions with TortoiseGit are used with the context menu of internet explorer.
- SourceTree
  - SourceTree is a free Git client for Windows and Mac that simplifies how you interact with your Git repositories. SourceTree is very simple for beginners to use because it eliminates the Git command line. It is also very powerful for advanced users with many features to allow them to be more productive.

Other Tools

Code Tools and IDEs

IDEs (Integrated Development Environments) are software applications that provide developers with the ability for comprehensive software development in one program. They normally have a source code editor, automation tools, and a debugger. Modern IDEs have intelligent code completion that save you many keystrokes when typing code. Some even have compilers, interpreters, or both. Version control systems are often integrated. Many ColdFusion developers take advantage of IDEs.

Using IDEs helps keep CF alive by maintaining a friendly work environment. This can encourage new developers to work with CF. They also save time when coding.

These are some of the most popular IDEs used by CFers according to the *State of the CF Union 2018* survey.

- Sublime
  - Sublime is a cross platform source code editor and IDE with a Python API. It natively supports many programming and markup languages including CFML. There are many user created plugins with great community support and 48.5% of all CFers who responded to the State of the CF Union survey use Sublime Text 3.
- CF Builder
  - CF Builder is Adobe's flagship IDE for ColdFusion. Released for CF 2016, it was designed to help you develop, debug, test, and deploy applications faster and 20% of all CFers in the State of the CF Union survey use it. Now with the new CF 2018 version, many new features have been implemented such as:
    - Intelligent Code Assist
    - Professional Coding Support
    - Security Code Analyzer

■ Improved Integrated Debugger

- Dreamweaver
  - Dreamweaver is another IDE by Adobe, more geared to graphic designers and HTML site development. It was created in 1997, so it's almost as old as ColdFusion and many CFers started out with it. It used to have CFML support built in but recently that was removed. Fortunately you can add it back in yourself.
  - 18% of all CFers who responded to the State of the CF Union survey use it. You can build, edit, and view CF code within Dreamweaver. It combines a virtual design surface known as Live View and a code editor. It comes with an array of features including:
    - ■ Syntax Highlighting
    - ■ Code Completion
    - ■ Code Collapsing
    - ■ Real Time Syntax Checking
    - ■ Code Introspection
- Visual Studio Code
  - This Open Source IDE by Microsoft (with downloads for macOS, Windows and Linux) has become popular in the last two years. It has a lot of plugins to integrate different technologies such as Git and Linter for CF. You can even run CommandBox and use Code Completion for ColdFusion. Or if you use the ColdBox Framework, you can easily insert boilerplate code. You can find more suggestions on how to us VSC for ColdFusion development at commandbox.ortusbooks.com/ide-integrations/visual-studio-code

Code Reuse

Some developers minimize their use of newly created code. Instead, they simply change parameters and call it from other parts of the app. This allows for tried and true code to be used to save time. This is not a direct copy/paste method though. That would duplicate code and make for maintenance headaches. Code is reused using CFC functions or even the more old fashioned CFINCLUDE. Any of the MVC frameworks such as FW/1, ColdBox or FuseBox make code reuse and code organization easy. This increases your productivity and saves on maintenance time.

Related Podcast: Best Practices Are Best, Except When They're Not with Nolan Erck

Monitoring Tools

CF Server Monitoring tools can help maintain CF alive by giving you the best chance of early detection of performance issues, failures, and security issues. The number one monitoring tool to use for CF is FusionReactor.

FusionReactor is a Java based performance monitor which is used to monitor in particular ColdFusion, Lucee, and Railo. FusionReactor features include:

- Gathering Metrics inside Servers
- Viewing Stack Traces
- Resource Graphs
- Crash Protection
- FR Mobile for iOS and Android
- Production Debugger
- Production Java Profiler

CF 2018 comes with a built in server monitoring tool, but it doesn't have all the features of FusionReactor.

Caching Solutions

A major measure of performance for the Web is how fast content is delivered to users. As web traffic increases, data delivery times usually increase too. Caching is a strategy used to minimize slow pages.

The number one solution for ColdFusion users is EHCache. EHCache is actually built into ColdFusion. It is used for CFCache tags, cache get, and cache put functions. It is notable to mention that Lucee has a bit more than that. They have a caching mechanism that creates multiple named caches that point to an internal or external data storage.

Caching solutions keep CF alive by boosting performance, offloading work from your database server, and simplifying your scalability issues.

Build REST APIs and Microservices

Keep CF alive by building REST APIs. Many developers are now building REST APIs and there should be no reasons CF cannot do the same. A REST (Representational State Transfer) API defines a set of functions where requests can be performed and responses received via HTTP protocol. They are compatible with CFML and very easy to test. The top reason ColdFusion users used to use REST APIs was if they wanted to integrate with a third party code.

Now, CFers can make applications that any technological platform can touch via full-bodied traditional apps. However, most CFers who develop REST APIs do it from homegrown sources and only for their own websites. New applications such as ColdBox allow for a great leap forward when it comes to REST APIs. Pretty much all CFers are using REST APIs now with some form of application. These are normally much better than anything you can write on your own.

> *"...we're really doing some modern things and using up to date ColdBox standards with MVC. We're doing a lot of RESTful APIs. We're doing some of these cutting edge things and it really makes it enjoyable and I've been really impressed with how ColdFusion has kept up with that, and how it's led the way on some of those things"*
> - Scott Coldwell, Developer and Sysadmin at Computer Know How

From CF Alive episode, "017 Managing an international team, Git, CFML, Node, Joomla, Headaches and Heartaches, with Scott Coldwell"

Related Podcast: The Best REST You've ever Had: ColdBox REST with Nathaniel Francis

CommandBox

"CFML is a fun and productive language and now with CommandBox,that productivity has gone sky high! I can run servers, copy configurations, wrap up and containerize applications easily. CommandBox has really changed how we run, build and deploy apps, all using the same language."

-Mark Drew, Director at Charlie Mike Delta

From CF Alive episode, "035 Getting started fast with Docker, with Mark Drew"

According to the State of the CF Union 2018, CommandBox is used by 80% of CFers polled. With all this fuss, what is CommandBox? CommandBox is a standalone tool for the three major OS's-- Windows, Mac, and Linux, designed by Ortus Solutions. It is doing its part in keeping CF alive by providing a base that many other Box tools can operate with. It provides a CLI (Command Line Interface) designed for many purposes including:

- Developer Productivity
  - CommandBox has a Docker image for productivity and portability. This allows you to orchestrate live servers in multi-tier deployments.
- Tool Interaction
  - CommandBox has a REPL (Read-Evaluate-Print-Loop) console for immediate CFML interaction.

- Package Management
  - CommandBox also functions as a Package Management tool and integrates with ForgeBox, CommandBox's community of CF projects.
- Embedded CFML Servers
  - CommandBox has the ability to construct lightweight CFML servers (Adobe ColdFusion and Lucee) in any directory from the command line.
- Application Scaffolding
  - CommandBox has a huge amount of commands for quickly constructing ColdBox/CommandBox/TestBox applications

It is integrated to work with any other Box product. CommandBox is great for CFML as well. In fact, it is extensible to any ColdFusion product. CommandBox is a true ColdFusion tool. Another great feature of CommandBox is its built-in help system. There is built-in help for every system command so you will always know what you are doing.

> *"CommandBox has changed the way I develop. It allows you to have a ColdFusion server running locally on your machine without the full install of ColdFusion, which can be a resource hog. If you're using CommandBox, you don't need to worry about that. The other wonderful thing about CommandBox is, I can install Lucee 4/5, Lucee 5, ColdFusion 9/2, ColdFusion 10, ColdFusion 11, ColdFusion 2016, and have all those servers running as a WAR file. If I have a beefy enough machine, I've ran two and three servers at the same time, had them all talking to each other."*

> - George Murphy, Software Design Engineer Manager, <u>Alion Science and Technology</u>

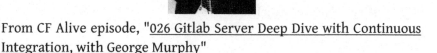

From CF Alive episode, "<u>026 Gitlab Server Deep Dive with Continuous Integration, with George Murphy</u>"

CommandBox is ever-changing and evolving. It is continuously adding more developments to its platform. A neat development to see would be for Twig support. Twig is the modern template engine for PHP. With more Twig support, CFers can use CommandBox to help bridge the gap between CFML and PHP.

"I'm proud to develop in ColdFusion, because it has the combination. Specifically, being a part of the ColdBox and a lot of the open source community as part of ColdFusion, because we have three things.

One, we have a great tradition. We have been a part of some of the greatest highs and a few of the lows of the web development history. Second, we've got some tenacity in there. A lot of the people who are very strong in the CFML community are people who have been doing this for a while and they've been doing it well. That's tenacity to not go from one thing, to the next thing, to the next thing, but really craft something solidly and well.

Third, we've got some of the most forward thinking, and highly developed, and amazing tools that we could imagine. We're going to be hanging out and Into The Box with the guy that invented CommandBox, as well as the guy that invented ColdBox itself. These are some just amazing tools that the CFML community has been blessed with.

I think we have the key parts that I would want in any community, tradition. We've got time honored tenacity and we've got some innovation, and forward thinking. That's exactly what I want to be a part of."

- Nathaniel Francis, Works at Computer Know How

From CF Alive episode, "008 The Best REST You've ever Had: ColdBox REST with Nathaniel Francis"

John Farrar believes that CommandBox education is paramount. He says that by teaching through CommandBox, new users will be more motivated to stay the course with CFML. The simplicity of CommandBox and its ability to set up servers immediately can be very motivating to beginning developers. He states that it is the best way to get new developers started with CF.

> *"...the honest easiest way I can introduce a new developer, is I say, 'Okay, bring me your computer, let's look for content on CommandBox.'*
>
> *They download it, and I just show them how to get a site set up with CommandBox. It is the drop dead simplest way to get a developer started. I think we need to introduce more people to CommandBox. I think we need to get more ColdFusion developers aware of it. When they look at it, and they spin up a server that fast and that easy.*
>
> *I like watching their mouth start to dry up. They're just sitting there with their jaw hanging. It's like, 'What did you do?' It's like, 'You saw everything, that was it.' 'But you didn't download the server.' I said, 'No, it's running in Lucee.' It actually did, it's in the Box package, and the way it pulls it. I said, 'That's just how long it takes.' They're like, 'Huh?'"*

- John Farrar, CEO, <u>SOSensible Group</u>

From CF Alive episode, "<u>018 VUE More With Less, with John Farrar</u>"

Frameworks and Methodology

"What's it like being a new ColdFusion developer, versus many of the other people in the community who've been doing it for 10, 15 years? I only started programming about five years ago. When I got to my first job, ColdFusion was the language they had just started using. It was a brand new development team. All of us were pretty new at it. They had picked ColdFusion. I didn't know any better. I didn't know any different, I

guess I should say. I started using it. It was our own, homegrown something. I'm not even gonna call it a framework. I know that my team listening would agree with that.

There was a time where I got to the point developing on it that, I just wished that we had something else, because I could look into some other communities, and see all the tooling they had, all the packages, or modules that they had to share, and see how we were feeling like we were doing everything from scratch. It's just kind of the feeling like you hear ColdFusion is dying, and I remember subscribing to that belief."
- Eric Peterson, CFML and Javascript developer at O.C. Tanner in Salt Lake City, Utah

From CF Alive episode, "023 Modules Make Your Projects Have Superpowers, with Eric Peterson"

Code Frameworks

"We're also seeing a lot of people on the other end of the spectrum who are what I'd call the legacy ColdFusion developers: people who learned how to use ColdFusion in maybe 2000, or 2001. They learned how to use the CF include tag and maybe custom tags, and they kind of stopped learning at that point. They're not doing object oriented development, they're not following best practices, they're not using MVC frameworks."
- Nolan Erck, Owner and Chief Consultant at South of Shasta Consulting

From CF Alive episode, "059 Migrating legacy CFML to MVC (Model View Controller) with Nolan Erck"

According to the <u>State of the ColdFusion Union 2018</u>, most CFers prefer a homegrown code framework. But, the most commonly used third-party code framework application is ColdBox (followed by FW/1 and Fusebox respectively). There are a few advantages of using a third party framework over a homegrown system. For example, you can save time and resources by using a third-party app. Also, third-party apps are already tried and tested and are regularly updated with new features and bug fixes. Plus if you have problems, there are many other CFers you can ask about how do a particular thing in that framework.

> *"There's a lot of web development still being done in ColdFusion where the developers are just using old technology – CF includes and custom tags and not a whole heck of a lot else. Either because they're scared to learn the new things, or they think it's going to be overly complicated. Maybe they think it's too many files, or too much code. Perhaps it doesn't actually solve the problem. Maybe they're just not aware of it either. There are a lot of people that just for whatever reason are not able to budget time and money to go to conferences and to learn what the current trends are. And I think we need to bridge that gap more and fix that problem. Let's take the people that are still writing code as if it's 2001, whether intentionally or otherwise, and help them improve. It's actually not that hard to go from your old CF to modern CF code.*
>
> *People that are still writing CF include based code, they don't really quite know how a FW/1, or ColdBox works and they need to go along those steps."*
>
> \- Nolan Erck, Owner and Chief Consultant
> at <u>South of Shasta Consulting</u>

From CF Alive episode, "<u>059 Migrating legacy CFML to MVC (Model View Controller) with Nolan Erck</u>"

Let's take a look at the most popular CF framework, ColdBox, and see what it can do for you. Code Frameworks help keep CF alive by saving CFers precious resources and making coding easier.

> *"Being willing to make the best of a tool that you know, rather than looking for the next silver bullet."*
>
> -Nathaniel Francis, <u>ColdBox Alliance Partner</u>

From CF Alive episode, "<u>008 The Best REST You've ever Had: ColdBox REST with Nathaniel Francis</u>"

ColdBox

So, what is ColdBox? ColdBox is a convention-based <u>HMVC</u> (Hierarchical Model View Controller) framework used specifically for CFML. It provides a team standard when working developmental projects. Also, it has a modular architecture. This allows for construction of hierarchical MVC apps instead of large applications. It is also incredibly easy to install especially if running CommandBox. All it takes is a simple one line command.

> *"Having done development in other languages, you just don't have the same convenience of all of those built in methods and then you add ColdBox on top of it and you've got all these other conventions and super tight methods you can leverage. With other languages, you find yourself reinventing the wheel over and over and over again to solve problems that were already solved in CFML many many years ago.*
>
> *For me it's let's find a language that gives me the best toolkit to start out with, the biggest tool box to work with, and if I have all of those tools and I have them readily available and conveniently assembled, then it makes it so much easier for me to quickly build and deploy powerful and bug free applications. So that's why I'm excited about CFML and I really continue to be because I think a lot of times the CFML development community can be it's own worst enemy, because we don't' spend enough*

time honing and looking at how we've done it this way for so many years, how can we do things differently. Or we're stuck in the java development model and we want to do things like java does them and we totally neglect the power of our loosely typed language and rapid application development, and how powerful it is in abstracting and scaffolding applications very quickly."

- Jon Clausen, President, Silo Web

From CF Alive episode, "011 Portable CFML with Cloud deployments, Microservices and REST with Jon Clausen"

Content Management Systems

A CMS (Content Management System) is a software application that helps to manage your digital content. This being said, having a good CMS is very important and makes CF more alive. Here's how content management can help any CF project.

- Update your Website on your own Terms
    - You no longer need to rely on third-party applications or hosts to update your web app. Simply update as you see fit.
- Extreme Ease of Use
    - No need to understand in-depth language programming to build a project. This is great for CF beginners learning to build their own web apps.
- Make Simple Changes without Full Redesign
    - A CMS will allow you to cherry-pick exactly what needs to be changed without doing a project overhaul.
- Access most up-to-date Web Design Features
    - Constant updates to the CMS will make sure you have the most modern availabilities for your application.

- Manage your Entire Marketing System
  - A good CMS will have tools for SEO, email marketing, social media marketing, and blogging. Some will even allow you to collect fees and donations, create event registration forms, and store member info.

ContentBox

"When I looked at what it took to do certain things with the ColdFusion language I was immediately struck by the simplicity of it. Just started building from there. It's just a great tool, great language, what I consider to be very direct in the way that you implement certain things. I think that's why we've seen the success in products like ColdBox, ContentBox over the years. The tools that we've put together. Just fell in love and I've loved building programs with ColdFusion ever since."

- Seth Engen, Co-owner of <u>Computer Know How</u>

From CF Alive episode, "<u>016 Adventures with ColdFusion and ContentBox in the Wild, with Seth Engen</u>"

ContentBox is an open-source modular CMS engine from Ortus Solutions that allows you to create websites, blogs, wikis, web apps, and RESTful web services. ContentBox can be deployed to any CFML engine or Java servlet container. It is built with an open-source MVC framework foundation (ColdBox). It is simple to install with one line on ComandBox's CLI. ContentBox also provides modularity. Using CommandBox and ForgeBox, you can install modules and extend your app in seconds. ForgeBox modules include themes, widgets, ColdBox modules, ContentBox modules, and more. A number of built-in interception points also come with ContentBox. Along with these features, ContentBox utilizes the use of CFCs (ColdFusion Components) due to its CFML abilities. On top of all this, ContentBox is Docker friendly. It has its own Docker image which can distribute to multiple replicas with ease. Here are a few benefits of combining Docker with ContentBox:

- Embedded Database or connect to any SQL database
- Image and Application Health Checks
- SSL Support
- Distributed caching
- Distributed sessions
- Data persistence
- Custom data mounts

As of June 2018, ContentBox 4.0 was released as its latest version. One of the major developments was that Lucee 5 now powers the CLI. All third-party libraries were also upgraded. These include:

- JGit
- Launch4J
- Runwar
- JLine 3

ContentBox has revamped its server logs and improved its task runner support. Those who use ContentBox believe that education of it is a key to making CF more alive. Ortus Solutions now has a sponsored education program for those wanting to learn Box tools.

> "CFML has never been more portable, it's never required fewer resources to run, for example, the ColdBox CMS ContentBox. I can run a content box instance very comfortably, day in and day out on 256Mb's of memory. Now when we're talking about the monolithic stuff, when was the last time where we had CFML deployments being comfortable on that small of a heap size. It's become much more portable and it's much more realistic to be able to deploy smaller and smaller resources on commodity hardware that just wasn't really an option."
>
> - Jon Clausen, President, Silo Web

From CF Alive episode, "011 Portable CFML with Cloud deployments, Microservices and REST with Jon Clausen"

Mura CMS

Some CFers use Mura as their CMS. Mura is one of the most mature ColdFusion CMS.

It is used by many companies including Scientific American magazine, Fidelity Worldwide Investment, Intuit, Zweifel, and NATO NSHQ.

Mura also hosts its own annual conference called MuraCon. This covers both Mura, ColdFusion and Marketing topics.

Preside

One CMS tool that CFers can use is Preside. Preside is an open source Enterprise class CMS application. It is a system focused on DX (designer/developer experience). The platform is designed to not get in the way of development and be as user-friendly as possible. Its MVC framework provides separation of visual design from function. The Java foundation allows for a proper Enterprise stack and scaling of your projects.

Preside is also multilingual and multi-site. This means you have the flexibility to store all or partial elements of your content and model the storage organization to fit your needs. Thousands of sites can be completely separate or share common content. You can use this to form part of a traditional web CMS or underpin a RESTful API.

JavaScript Libraries

A great way to enhance your CFML experience is to make use of JavaScript Libraries. Out of the CFers polled through the State of the CF Union 2018, over 90% use JQuery as their JS library of choice. Using JS libraries are very useful because they provide frameworks that can be used to help develop frontend code. Other common JS frameworks include React, Angular and Vue.

CSS Frameworks

CSS (Cascading Style Sheet) frameworks are prepared frameworks designed to allow for easier web design through the use of the CSS language. The most popular use of CSS framework among CF users is Bootstrap. There are many advantages for using Bootstrap depending on your application needs.

- It is easy to use and easy to get started with it.
- It has a useful grid system allowing you to build fixed and responsive grids. This can be very useful when dealing with mobile applications.
- For most elements of Bootstrap, they are based in HTML.
- Bootstrap contains a huge list of pre-styled components including:
  o Dropdowns
  o Button Groups
  o Navigation Bar
  o Breadcrumbs
  o Labels & Badges
  o Alerts
  o Progress Bars
- Bootstrap is built with bundled JavaScript plugins.
- New users can take full advantage of their extensive documentation system.

CFC Dependency Injection Frameworks and Tools

Dependency Injection (DI) frameworks help you create your CFC instances. They help inject references to other CFCs to help manage the relationships between them. Many CFers are using CFCs through a homegrown build. This is great for simpler applications but for more complex applications, DI frameworks are an enormous help. If you're using CFCs seriously, you may want to check out one of these dependency injection frameworks:

- WireBox
- DI/1
- ColdSpring

WireBox and DI/1 are actively maintained. ColdSpring has not seen any development in many years yet, many CFers still use it.

Persistence Frameworks

Most CFers don't seem to use ORM (Object Relational Mapping) frameworks. Yet users who have objects in their code seem to use the built-in ColdFusion ORM (Hibernate). These are not mutually exclusive however. For example, the ColdBox cborm module is actually a library you use along with ColdFusion ORM. Many major frameworks actually have their own version of ORM. ORM isn't an incredibly popular option in the ColdFusion community. CFers like their cfquery tags and don't want to let someone else's code manipulate their data. But using the ORM approach can speed up development and help make ColdFusion more alive.

Testing and Mocking Frameworks

The most popular testing framework is TestBox. It is the only maintained testing framework at this point but there are other frameworks available as well. Other choices for CFers include MXUnit and Selenium. If you have MXUnit tests you can import them into TestBox.

According to Brad Wood:

"When you start writing unit tests, you want to test a single function in isolation-- only the code in that function. If that function calls another function, you want to mock and have a fake function call, but it can call for you. Mocking is just a library that creates fake CFCs, fake functions, fake queries to fake a database call, basically used for creating mock data and mock interfaces so you can eliminate everything else but the code you're running the test on."

As of now, few CF users use Mocking Frameworks. MockBox is a good one and comes with TestBox. More CFers could be using mocking. Through the use of a mocking framework and automated testing, you can reduce the amount of time spent on debugging.

Mobile Development Frameworks

The vast majority of ColdFusion developers don't use any CF Mobile development framework. That is surprising. Mobile development is an integral part of today's development environment.

However, most developers who are doing mobile development are using PhoneGap. It is an Adobe product used for mobile development for iPhone and Android. It is an application container mobile apps using HTML, CSS, and JavaScript. PhoneGap is free and open-sourced under the Apache license.

A large chunk of CF developers doing mobile development also use the native iOS and Android tools.

Security Tools

Given the increasing number of high profile hacks on web servers these days, security is a top priority. Pete Freitag knows better than anyone. He is a security guru for Adobe ColdFusion. He created two tools that can be used to better secure your code and applications: HackMyCF and FuseGuard.

HackMyCF scans all your CF servers regularly and emails you a report on any out of date CF or JVM versions. And missing hotfixes. Or configuration security holes. It may scare you the first time you run it when you discover how many server security vulnerabilities that you have. After you have applied all the patches and config changes, you can rerun it to make sure everything is now up to date and secure.

FuseGuard is a ColdFusion specific Web Application Firewall (WAF) that protects against common hacker hacker exploits.

It inspects all web requests before your CFML code executes. If it spots a malicious request it can either log it or block continued execution completely. It stops all common CF hacker attacking including:

- Malicious File Uploads
- Remote Code Execution
- Cross Site Scripting (XSS)
- SQL Injection
- Session Hijacking
- Cross Site Request Forgery
- Path Traversal Attacks
- Null Byte Injection
- Password Dictionary Attacks
- CRLF Injection
- Malicious User Agents
- XML Entity Injection
- XML External DTD Injection

This is a godsend if you have old or insecure code that you haven't had time to fix yet. But don't rely only on a WAF because hackers are always evolving new exploits. So I recommend you prioritize reviewing your code for security vulnerabilities and remediating them. The new CF 2018 security tools are ideal for this.

Miscellaneous Frameworks and Tools

ColdFusion also has an array of miscellaneous tools to make your developing life easier. Two of these tools are LogBox and DocBox. LogBox is part of the Ortus Box family, but it is a standalone program. LogBox performs the same operations as CF Log but is much more flexible. You can dynamically provision where you want log messages to be logged to. If you are using Docker containers to run your apps, LogBox is very useful. Since there's no static files system underneath a container, it's important to be able to log your error messages outside of the container. DocBox is the oldest folk of the ColdDock project. It was acquired by Ortus and rebranded. It allows you to generate HTML documentation of your CFCs. These are just very helpful tools that you can use for your CF applications.

"I have been using ColdFusion (CFML) for last 7 years. It's useful for rapid development and it's easy to learn. It has got features, capabilities and frameworks which make a web language modern i.e. MVC Application Frameworks, Dependency Injection Frameworks, Testing Frameworks, Content Management Systems (CMS), CLI, Package Manager, and many more. CFML has a great community.

There are a number of CFML conferences every year which bring the community together and give opportunities to meet peers, experts and leaders and get to learn about the latest technologies, development methodologies, tools, and frameworks. CFML has become advanced language which can be recognized at par with any other latest web language."

- Uma Ghotikar, Web application developer at ICF

From CF Alive episode, "077 Fundamentals of Unit Testing, BDD and Mocking (using TestBox and MockBox) with Uma Ghotikar"

API Manager

"You also have API Manager that's there, that's a separate product. All of those are different and that's a new product in itself too, that's built from the ground up, separate installation and scale ability and all that built in just like we did with API Manager. So when you look at that and you just take a step back you'll see that ColdFusion is a technology toolset and it now has all of these different applications that are part of that toolset to enable developers in the modern day to do their work and do it quickly, vastly, reliably, securely and really do it and dependably."

- Elishia Dvorak, Technical Marketing Manager at Adobe

From CF Alive episode, "063 Adobe API Manager (the business case) + CF Summit sneak peak with Elishia Dvorak"

Nowadays, APIs are the core of programming and of ColdFusion. The close coupling that CF has is starting to take a back seat to APIs. This is why the use of API Managers will make ColdFusion more alive. With the release of ColdFusion 2016 Enterprise Edition, Adobe included the new API Manager. But due to the botched launch of CF 2016, nobody really knew it existed. Many users happened to stumble upon it while using CF 2016. Adobe did not do enough marketing with it. With the release of ColdFusion 2018, new features were added to the API manager. This time it was properly announced. We were glad to see Adobe improve its CF marketing.

An alternative to Adobe's API Manager is Taffy. Taffy is an API manager created by Alan Tuttle. Taffy is low friction and easy to start. It is both compatible with ColdFusion and Lucee. As a matter of fact, it is backwards compatible all the way to ColdFusion 8. Taffy prefers convention to configuration. It also has hardly any boilerplate code.

Related Podcast: What's New In CF 10, 11, And 2016 That You May Have Missed? with Charlie Arehart

Package Management Tools

CommandBox works amazingly well as a package manager for ColdFusion. You can use it to locate and install pre-written modules for you. Out of the box it works with ForgeBox and you can add other endpoints, such as Git, CFLib, RIAForge, HTTP, and local file/folder. When a package is installed, all of its dependencies are automatically installed for you too. Making using packages fast and easy.

This gives you a consistent and scriptable method to install the libraries you need in a simple manner. ForgeBox lets you configure your modules as easy to install packages

One request developers have is for a built-in ColdFusion Package Management tool. Neither Adobe or Lucee has this yet. They do listen to the community. Together we can help keep CF alive by focusing on more integrated tools for the platform

ForgeBox

"Programming languages are sustained by the community of developers that use them. The growth and relevance of ColdFusion depend on its users fostering this community - by embracing change, sharing knowledge, and contributing to open source projects."

-Matthew Clemente, Founding Partner at <u>Season 4</u>

From CF Alive episode, "<u>055 send.Better() – Giving ColdFusion Email a REST with Matthew Clemente</u>"

ForgeBox is one of the greatest tools developed for those who use ColdFusion. It is a software repository and directory that you can either use manually or with CommandBox. On ForgeBox, you can find user created software packages. There are many different types of packages available. These include:

- <u>ContentBox Modules</u>
- <u>CommandBox Modules</u>
- <u>CFWheels Plugins</u>
- <u>ContentBox Themes</u>
- <u>MVCs</u>
- <u>Preside Extensions</u>

Also if you need help modularizing your code, the users on ForgeBox can help. There are apps on there that will help you to do so. If you create app or modules that will help others then share them! No need for excessive work to be done if something simple as been created to help. Another place to discuss ForgeBox modules is on the CF Slack channel. Be sure to sign up there if you haven't already done so.

> *"If you have some code that you're using for project to project, wrap it up in a module, and push it up to ForgeBox. If you need help, you can come talk in the ColdFusion Slack, specifically the box products channel. There's a lot of us that hang out there that can help you modularize your code."*

> - Eric Peterson,
> CFML and Javascript developer at <u>O.C. Tanner</u> in Salt Lake City, Utah

From CF Alive episode, "<u>023 Modules Make Your Projects Have Superpowers, with Eric Peterson</u>"

What is really needed is for people to keep creating modules and sharing them. The best modules are specific and practical.

> *"Cleansing of phone formats, right. Phone formats across the world always should actually be plus date, plus country code and something else right. Write something that turns any stupid number into a properly formatted telephone number. Add that to ForgeBox and everyone will be using that. Don't make it something you have to Google and go to various different websites to find what their proper widget is."*

> -Mark Drew, Director at <u>Charlie Mike Delta</u>

From CF Alive episode, "<u>035 Getting started fast with Docker, with Mark Drew</u>"

Another great feature would be recommending popular modules during ForgeBox setup and startup. This can make sure everybody has the best that the CF community can offer. By acting as a community during active developing, we can ensure CF stays alive.

"Of course, it's good to know that I'm a part of building the ecosystem, the open source projects out there that are shared on GitHub and shared on ForgeBox and the great thing about that is that everybody can be proud to be part of the open source ecosystem. That's not a secret club that you have to be in or there's no barrier to entry. Anyone who writes a reusable function or module and they stick it out on ForgeBox and they publish the code, they can also be proud to be part of building the open source communities."

-Brad Wood,
Software Architect and Platform Evangelist Ortus Solutions

From CF Alive episode, "<u>029 Design Patterns for amazing app architecture (16 patterns), with Brad Wood</u>"

Related Podcast: <u>CommandBox + ForgeBox: ColdFusion Code, Package, Share, Go! with Luis Majano</u>

Summary

- Use Docker Containerization for more reliable, scalable and secure apps.
- Use CommandBox as a CLI and package manager for CF.
- Use Source Control such as Git.
- Use Sublime Text 3 or CF Builder CF IDEs to save development time.

- Use FusionReactor CF monitoring tool to reduce server slowdowns and crashes.
- Use frameworks such as ColdBox, FW/1 to organize your code and save time.
- Use a CF CMS such as ContentBox, Mura or Preside if your app manages user content.
- Start doing automated testing and mocking using TestBox and MockBox
- Use security tools HackMyCF and FuseGuard to decrease hacker risks
- If you create APIs then use the CF API manager for better control and uptime.
- Share your programming success. Be active in the community and contribute to ForgeBox.

Let's look at how we can share the success of CF with others in the next chapter on Outreach.

CHAPTER 4

Outreach

"Technology no longer consists just of hardware or software or even services, but of communities. Increasingly, community is a part of technology, a driver of technology, and an emergent effect of technology."

-Howard Rheingold, Author of <u>Smart Mobs</u>

Despite its great technological features, ColdFusion is only as strong as its community. Nobody should feel alone when coding in CF any more when there is a vibrant CF Community you can be part of. That is why outreach to developers outside the community is so important. Together, we can help to solve issues, learn new features, and create better code for the future. Without active CF experts and developers in a community, ColdFusion wouldn't be really alive.

What Would It Take to have a happy, healthy ColdFusion developers community?

There are several factors we need to address to strengthen the community. This doesn't mean growing the number of people alone. We should also strengthen the resolve of the community, share CF knowledge and reduce negativity. A collective effort of the entire CF ecosystem will help make this happen. So how will we learn what to do? Let's get educated.

Education

"Develop a passion for learning. If you do, you will never cease to grow."
-Anthony J. D'Angelo

Education is the foundation for the current development of the CF community. It is also the basis for the future of the ColdFusion platform. Most CF experts and developers will agree on one thing: no matter how much you know, there is always something to learn. There are always new CF improvements, development methods, and tools.

So, what measures can be taken to improve education throughout the CF community? First, developers can start by improving our own knowledge.

ColdFusion training resources

A good place to start adding to your ColdFusion education is this list of CF training resources

1. Adobe ColdFusion Developer Center
2. Adobe ColdFusion Blog
3. Adobe YouTube
4. CF Alive Podcast
5. Learn CF In A Week
6. Lynda
7. Ortus Solutions
8. Ortus Solutions YouTube
9. TeraTech YouTube
10. Charlie Arehart
11. FigLeaf Software
12. Accelebrate
13. Roundpeg

Related article Comprehensive ColdFusion training list (17 resources).

Set Learning Goals

"Education is a big thing. We need to make it easy for people to get moved over."

- Gavin Pickin,
Software Consultant for Ortus Solutions, Corp

From CF Alive episode, "010 All things ContentBox (new API, ContentStore, Themes and more) with Gavin Pickin"

There is a world of CF information out there to learn. No one person can know everything. All CF experts and beginners alike all have areas in which they can improve their knowledge and that's OK. There is nothing shameful about lacking knowledge on different topics. Some of the most powerful words are "I don't know" and "can you help me". They allow us a chance to grow through learning. This, in turn, strengthens developers and the community as a whole.

First, developers should discover and admit where their weaknesses are. Practicing mastered skills alone does not promote growth of self. Once you establish direction, developing a time frame and goals are next. Writing down goals is one of the most helpful things a developer can do. Developers should write down their dreams and then set realistic short-term goals to reach them.

For Example:

- END TARGET GOAL:
  o Master the art of using Docker.
- YEAR-END GOAL:
  o Attend the next DockerCon as a Speaker.
- MONTHLY GOAL:
  o Create a new application using different areas of Docker at the beginning of every month.

- WEEKLY GOAL:
  - o Focus on a particular area of Docker and learn as much as possible. Compose a brief article on that area and post on your blog.
- DAILY GOAL:
  - o Practice newly acquired skills.

Written goals should not stay tucked away in a notebook either. Print them out and put next to your monitor. Or make a background image from them for your laptop and phone.

Having a clear vision path for goals does more than remind; it also motivates and inspires. By watching your goals accomplished, you develop a sense of pride in what you do. Get excited when you finish a step. Celebrate your daily goals with that extra scoop of ice cream for dessert. Yearly goals could have a much bigger celebration. Remember, it is OK to reward yourself for hard work. Along with this, share your success. This can motivate others in the community to do what you have done.

Never stop learning. A route you may choose to take is to become a specialist. There is always a need for an expert. Sometimes it feels good to be the one thought of when answers are needed. Give back to the community. In ColdFusion when people think of security, Pete Freitag immediately comes to mind. For a veteran CFML troubleshooter, you need to look no farther than Charlie Arehart. Through continuous learning and practice, anybody can become one of the greats.

Teaching about ColdFusion

So you have mastered the art of learning, now what? Do something good with your knowledge, TEACH! Here are some ways you can teach in the CF community:

- Help others in the CF Slack channel.
- Blog about what you have learned.
- Go on the CF Alive podcast.

- Speak at a <u>CF conference</u>.
- Share your ideas in the "hallway track" at a conference

"I think the reason I'm proud to use ColdFusion is because I have an opportunity to give back. I think if you are feeling stuck in ColdFusion, if you're feeling like it's dying, I would wager a guess that it's because you're not utilizing the community. You're not going to them for help. You're not going to them for modules, and you're not giving back the things that you've learned. Because in my experience, that changed everything for me. I went from wanting to, trying to convince my team that we should move to a completely different language, to just loving what we were doing. We've been able to modernize in place, and bring our code more up to date, and it keeps getting better every day. So it's exciting to code in our applications now, and in ColdFusion."

- Eric Peterson, CFML and Javascript developer

at <u>O.C. Tanner</u> in Salt Lake City, Utah

From CF Alive episode, "<u>023 Modules Make Your Projects Have Superpowers, with Eric Peterson</u>"

What you can do to further those around you and the next generation of CFers is astounding. Think back to the times when you were first starting out with ColdFusion. Everybody starts from the same place. Zero. Teachers have built the CF community by creating the developers that make it up today.

"I love the language. It was the first language I learned. I learned it because I was a musician and I needed a more efficient solution to managing our mailing list. So I went to a friend and said, "I need a mailing list! I'm tired of carrying this big folder where people put in their emails," and my friend said, "Well, you know there's this language called ColdFusion that has a cfquery tag, a cfoutput tag, and a cfmail tag," and I was in love. That's the truth. I have worked in other languages over the

years and although I do like all of them, when I need to get a real quick idea out, ColdFusion just seems to make it really simple to do. There's a lot of value in that and it has a great community. People might roll their eyes here and there, but I believe it's a great language to this day, and it has a lot of potential."

-Giancarlo Gomez,
Owner of CrossTrackr, Inc and Fuse Developments, Inc. and Senior Web Application Developer at Duty Free Americas

From CF Alive episode, "001 Amazing Adventures with CF WebSockets with Giancarlo Gomez"

CF teachers have the most important task in maintaining ColdFusion's survival. Passing along knowledge of CF. To be forgotten is to be lost. Sharing knowledge with the next generation of developers keeps ColdFusion alive. This knowledge ensures the survival of the platform and ushers in a new wave of improvements. We can complete another principal task of education, which is creating more teachers for the next generation.

"So at Ortus we're actually working on Ortus University, we're making courses for new developers as well as how to convert from other languages over to try and make it easier for them."

- Gavin Pickin, Software Consultant for Ortus Solutions, Corp

From CF Alive episode, "010 All things ContentBox (new API, ContentStore, Themes and more) with Gavin Pickin"

Be More Vocal about CF

Another thing that must change is the general mindset of the development community. Like many things in life, there is a lot of negativity that revolves around ColdFusion. "ColdFusion is dead." "Java is better than ColdFusion." "People who use ColdFusion are outdated." First off, these aren't true. Yet, these statements from outsiders can get under your skin. It produces a sense of shame in some ColdFusion developers. Why would you be ashamed of ColdFusion? It is a platform that has been making continuous breakthroughs over 20+ years. Nothing is embarrassing about that. With the release of CF 2018, there are a wave of performance and security upgrades. According to Tridib Roy Chowdhury, Adobe has reached its quarterly CF sales goals over the past 8 years. They have also experienced an annual average of 6-7% growth. There is no reason to be ashamed. Be proud of your platform.

"Stop being scared of bringing up CFML in the larger IT communities."

- Jon Clausen, President, <u>Silo Web</u>

From CF Alive episode, "<u>011 Portable CFML with Cloud deployments, Microservices and REST with Jon Clausen</u>"

Not only be proud of ColdFusion, but spread the word. Some people notice CF markers in URLs, and their reactions are far from enthusiastic. They can even be somewhat condescending. Don't sit by and accept it. Use positive reinforcement of CF to make your point. Show happiness. Say, "Wow! ColdFusion, huh? Who would have thought that after all this time CF would have the power to remain relevant? It might be a pretty decent platform..." Watch the disbelievers reaction after that. It may turn out that they don't know that much about ColdFusion and CFML. Here's your opportunity to educate. Boast about ColdFusion and be proud of your platform. You may find a CFML convert or someone who can acknowledge CF's power in programming today.

> *"For ColdFusion developers, what new ColdFusion technology or library you're going to have a chance to dip into, are you going to learn? I think that will help make ColdFusion better, make ColdFusion more alive and it will make the developers doing ColdFusion more proud of what they do. When you talk to another developer that's not a ColdFusion developer, you could more proudly talk to them about the modern practices that you're doing and not have to be ashamed of the legacy ColdFusion app that you managed that was written like it's 1999, right?"*

-Brad Wood,
Software Architect and Platform Evangelist Ortus Solutions

From CF Alive episode, "028 Design Patterns for amazing app architecture (16 patterns), with Brad Wood"

Start a Blog

A final step you can take is to start a blog. Many CF experts are already doing so. This is your opportunity to share anything you want about CF to an immense audience. No need to let anything slip by. New version releases are always a great read. Many CFers learn about the new features from blogs. Older versions are great to read about as well. It is good to see the mistakes made and how they were solved. Those who do not learn history are doomed to repeat it, right? Trace back your platform's programming roots. See the struggles it has overcome to find a deeper appreciation for CF today. The most popular of blog posts are the "How to" articles. These can provide help for the everyday CFer and provide info to guide them through tasks. Others prefer reading interviews with CF and programming experts. These interviews can provide real insight into ColdFusion functions and future. Also, readers love to see their questions answered. Create a comment block and respond to those who do comment. Engaging readers in a conversation about CF helps keep it alive.

"Talk about it, blog about it. Use it for applications. Go on CF Alive podcast and talk to Michaela Light and tell it how great it is. We have loads of people saying how bad it is and how old fashioned and old code and whatever. Tell them it's not true and why it's not true. Because the ones that are using it heavily know that it is not true, and that we are trying to keep the language as modern as possible and improve it."

-Gert Franz, CTO Rasia Switzerland &
Senior Solutions Architect at Helsana Versicherungen AG

From CF Alive episode, "024 CFML Debugging Jedi Tricks and Templates, with Gert Franz"

"A good goal for people to set is what's the new thing you're going to learn this year, what's the new thing you're going to learn this month, or this week, even if learning just means reading some blog post on Docker so it's a bit more demystified. You always have to be continually learning new things to keep yourself up to date on a topic."

-Brad Wood,
Software Architect and Platform Evangelist Ortus Solutions

From CF Alive episode, "028 Design Patterns for amazing app architecture (16 patterns), with Brad Wood"

Developer Outreach

One thing in ColdFusion is quite certain: without developers to use it, CF will die. To continue the survival and growth of CF, we must find developers and reach out. Developers comprise the heart and soul of ColdFusion.

What Would It Take to grow a strong developer base?

Start Early

Sometimes, it can be difficult to find CFML developers compared to other languages. So the only logical thing to do is to start making developers. All across the country, recruiters visit high schools. Military recruiters. College recruiters. Sports program recruiters. So why not software development ambassadors? There are students that realize that we are in the Age of Information. Software engineers and developers are paramount to the future of humanity. These students need that chance. Both Adobe, Lucee and the ColdFusion community can help with that.

One way to do this could be for an Adobe CF ambassador team to pursue students as future developers. A few simple permissions is all that it takes to go out and do it. This team could go to high school computer classes and pitch ColdFusion. They should bring along small mementos to hand out. These can be pens and magnets embossed with Adobe ColdFusion logos. This action can allow CF to be imprinted in students as a viable option for programming. They should evangelize the benefits of ColdFusion. Explain why ColdFusion is the right programming language for them. They should speak about the joys of developer life in an exciting way. Present the students with challenges and rewards for completing them. Express the joys of code creation and how fulfilling it is to see that creation come to life. Another option would be to offer a scholarship program. Adobe is already starting work on scholarship options. Yet, an active boost from the CF community would help in a big way. By helping students to pursue their dreams, students can help keep CF alive for the years to come in return.

High school isn't the only place this team should travel. Time to head back to college. College recruiting requires a whole new strategy. Small trinkets are fine to hand out, but they won't have the same hold. Also, college students tend to know what they want in a career path.

"To make ColdFusion more alive, I wish it gets included in the academic courses at schools and universities."

- Uma Ghotikar, Web application developer at ICF

From CF Alive episode, "077 Fundamentals of Unit Testing, BDD and Mocking (using TestBox and MockBox) with Uma Ghotikar"

Recruit college students

As with high schools, the team would need to make a physical appearance. Coordinating with department heads and professors would be necessary. This is much more lax than high school permissions. The team should prepare a professional yet entertaining presentation. This could include powerpoints, lectures, and basic software demonstrations. One benefit to recruiting at colleges is the volume of students. Each class usually is much larger than those at the high school level. This can help spread the CF message to a wider base of individuals. Another way of grabbing interest can be done at colleges by extracurricular seminars. Get permission to host a paid seminar at the college. These seminars could be held in collegiate convention centers and be open to the public. Be sure to set out some light snacks for attendees.

The best thing to offer at a college recruitment center is help with job placement. Adobe could offer entry-level development jobs for those who can meet preset qualifications. Along with Adobe, other ColdFusion affiliated companies should arrive as well. Let the students know some companies are in need of ColdFusion developers. It is becoming more difficult to find viable career paths. By holding a CF job fair, students will recognize ColdFusion as a name they trust. Adobe could also sponsor ColdFusion training for those who meet their hiring criteria. This would further motivate collegiate students to enter the ColdFusion community.

An advantage to recruiting at colleges is the network built between educators and CF. Adobe has started a continuing education program already. It relies on passive recruitment though. Students introducing Adobe to the colleges. With an active recruiting system, the number of ColdFusion users would rise. This could also allow CF to become a part of the curriculum at some institutions.

> *"Community's important. The events are important. I think it's also Adobe that's also going to put the word out and try and spread some of the ColdFusion message potentially at more at universities so where more people at work studying computer science. Maybe get some exposure to ColdFusion and that they see that actually it is a great language. I'm sure that would help. Obviously we're very strongly behind ColdFusion. We're supporting Adobe CF, Railo and Lucee."*
>
> - David Tattersall, Co-founder, Integral

From CF Alive episode, "022 FusionReactor Application Performance Monitor – Why It's Different Than Other APM Tools and What's New in Version 7 & the CLOUD, with David Tattersall"

Related Article: Comprehensive ColdFusion training list (16 resources)

Local Outreach

Adobe doesn't need to be the only one looking though. The CF community needs to step up their game on outreach. One easy way to do this is to start close to home. Develop a local club for ColdFusion. Facebook groups or Meetup.com are great platforms for this. Starting new user groups for CF is only the beginning. Leaders of the group should come together to hold meet and greets. These meet and greets do not need to be about ColdFusion. Get together with other CFers and grab some pizza and beer. Or hold a Lunch and Learn meeting during the day. Get to know each other and make some friends. The topic of ColdFusion is bound to show up anyway. Find out what you can about your fellows' CF experiences. This is keeping CF alive in the truest sense of the word.

> *"I've been an avid CFer from 2008 and it's been one awesome journey. From organizing meetups to building awesome applications, it's been great. The contributions to the community has been awesome too."*
> - SaravanaMuthu J, Founder & CTO at MitrahSoft

From this point, there are many different avenues for keeping CF alive in the local arena.

- Construct a website for your club together (using CFML of course). Or conduct other joint projects together.
- Do charitable works as a club and get the positivity of CF out into the public.
- Encourage friendly competitions and hackathons.

Make it fun to be part of the CF community! Throw mini CF conventions and have your club members each speak on a topic. Invite guest CF experts to come in and headline. When attending large conventions, raise money to go as a group. Showcase your CF pride!

"CF Life is always a great Joy."
- SaravanaMuthu J, Founder & CTO at <u>MitrahSoft</u>

Go Big or Go Home

"On the business side, we are really comfortable, we are very happy where it is. And that gives us you know like added incentive and possibly a little bit of headroom for us to kind of sit back and say, 'You know like can we do something really big? Can we do something adventurous?'"
- Tridib Roy Chowdhury, General Manager and Senior Director of Products at <u>Adobe Systems</u>

From CF Alive episode, "<u>065 The Future of ColdFusion (it is Bright) with Tridib Roy Chowdhury</u>"

After conquering the local areas of CF, let's think big now. There are some good ways to do this. A simple and effective methods is through CF podcasts. Podcasts can be great for interviews, presentations and simple stories involving CF. You don't have to get deeply technical unless you want to.

Webinars are great for showing code and slides and more tech details. Zoom is a great webinar platform for this, and is free for upto 40 minutes. Let's get some motivated speakers and evangelists for free webinars. Invite the public and fellow CFers. Start the CF revolution online! For best results, this should supported by the CF Community and sponsored by Adobe and Lucee. Any community event sponsored by the makers of CF will only hold that much more credence.

Another great way to reach out is via live stream events. These can be held on platforms such as FB Live, Periscope, Twitch and YouTube Live. To make these events effective, they must be planned out and announced a few weeks ahead of time. Get the crowd motivated. Next, find some of the great veteran CFers to be the presenters. Next, hold a livestream Q&A session with the hosts. This would be a fun and interactive way to get the community involved.

Hold Reddit AMAs. AMA on Reddit stands for Ask Me Anything. This is where someone will go onto Reddit, explain who they are, and open up the floor for questions. These are rapid-fire questions that the original poster (OP) will answer as many of as possible. These questions may be professional in nature or not. There is an entire group dedicated to this concept. This could help for ColdFusion exposure. For veterans, this could be a place to talk shop. Intermediate users may seek help for complicated issues. Beginners can learn tips and tricks on starting out. These forums are also available and seen by those outside of the community. Someone is bound to ask, "What is ColdFusion? Why should I use it?" This would then be the OP's time to shine and drive home how great ColdFusion is.

AMAs can also be hosted on Twitter. Or just have a theme and special hashtag for a TweetStorm hour.

> "I think I'm certainly looking forward to being able to share knowledge. I'm a bit believer in the phrase, when you teach you learn. I always find that I walk away energized from teaching as well. At the same time, there's a lot of great sessions out there, I look forward to sharing knowledge, just going to conferences where you get a chance to connect with peers and walk away re-energized about your work. As developers know, there's a lot of days that you're just slogging through lines and lines of code and some days it's not fun.
>
> I find that the energy that I get from there also keeps me energized throughout the corresponding months when I'm working on maybe some of those things that aren't as fun."
>
> - Jon Clausen, President, Silo Web

From CF Alive episode, "011 Portable CFML with Cloud deployments, Microservices and REST with Jon Clausen"

Hiring

One of the largest concerns with ColdFusion is the difficulty that some companies have with hiring CF developers. In our recent State of CF Union Survey 56% of respondents said that it's difficult for them to find CF developers. And yet 25% of CF developers say it is difficult to find CF work.

Clearly there is some kind of mismatch going on here. Perhaps the companies and developers are looking in the wrong places for CF jobs. Maybe the demand is in certain cities and the developers are in other cities. Or the companies require employees to work in their office every day while the developers prefer remote working. Or the companies need junior CF developers and they can only find senior ones with higher salaries than they budgeted.

Some of the solutions to hiring good CF developers include:

- Post the job in the CF Slack jobs sub-channel or in CF social media groups (in addition to traditional job boards)
- Use LinkedIn to search for candidates with ColdFusion experience or post LI ads
- Be open to remote work for the position
- Be ready to hire good developers from other languages and train them in CF.

This last point is something that two top CF companies, Pixl8 and Ortus Solutions, do. It can be done in a few weeks as ColdFusion is so easy to learn. And to be honest the core concepts of programming and object oriented development are the same in many languages. It is just that CFML is more efficient for coding them.

"We don't hire ColdFusion developers, it's very very rare that a new coldfusion developer starts working for us. Our model is that we take bright computer science people and you may have come from another MVC background and we train them up on Preside. I think what's really exciting is when you see a Rails developer getting excited about something using ColdBox."

-Alex Skinner, Founder <u>Pixl8</u>

From CF Alive episode, "<u>019 A Whirlwind Tour of Preside Application Framework in the Wild, with Alex Skinner</u>"

Bringing New Developers into the Community

"I think that case is very strong compared to other environments. The biggest one I see is people say is, "Well, I can't get developers". I just told you I could get a ColdFusion person up and running in ColdFusion in a week. So that argument about developers is dead."

- Thomas Grobicki, CEO of <u>Avilar Technologies, Inc</u>

From CF Alive episode, "<u>041 The true ROI of ColdFusion (How to Sell CF to your Boss or Client) with Thomas Grobicki</u>"

Once there are a high number of new developers, the next logical step is to welcome them into the community. To streamline this and increase retention, incoming developers need a place to go. One good step would be to create a home base for newcomers with a community website. This would be a centralized location for all CFers. The website could be broken down into separate forums and groups. Skill levels and specializations make for good criteria. This would navigate newer CFers to similar peers. A defined home base would allow easier outreach to CF experts for education purposes. Another simple way to organize the community would be through the use of CF Slack channel and Social Media. We could just add links to those groups from the community website.

Active Searching and Needs Development

Many other CF developers are in the community that are not in any groups. Why should they be left out? The answer is... they shouldn't. Active searching is needed to find these individuals. Searching social media platforms could help boost the ranks of the CF community. Forums and blog posts comment section also can turn up real connections. Get engaged with the community. Have conversations and talk about ColdFusion.

"Become more active in the community."

- Esmeralda Acevedo,
Software Consultant for Ortus Solutions, Corp

From CF Alive episode, "015 Better ContentBox Themes and Easily Creating an Amazing UI, with Esmeralda Acevedo"

Remember, when having these conversations keep in mind that every individual is unique. These individuals come from all walks of life. Treat everybody you come across with respect. The CF community is bright and colorful and filled with many different types of people. Young and old, men and women, LGBTQ, and races from all over the world. That is one of many things that makes the ColdFusion community great. Acceptance. Let's keep it that way.

On top of all this, a great way to maintain community retention is to cater to developer needs. As mentioned before, a prime way of doing this is to create subgroups. Some developers need a basics group to help them acclimate to ColdFusion. Others need more specialized topics such as integrating Box tools or Docker. There are many levels of ColdFusion. By covering as many of these topics as possible, we can be sure that we reach out to everybody's needs.

> *"Almost all the speakers, there's just little nuggets of wisdom and those little nuggets to me, I just come back and it's like where can I use this, number one? And number two, what is the benefit to the other members of the team? I subscribe a lot to Simon Sinek's approach, Leaders Eat Last. When I'm going, I'm looking because I know our team, we've developed a friendship. I know this is for this person, focus is this person's newer, this person's not yet acquainted with this. It's how are they introducing this? How can I show them this concept so it's easier to adapt to?"*

- John Farrar, CEO, <u>SOSensible Group</u>

From CF Alive episode, "<u>018 VUE More With Less, with John Farrar</u>"

The best way to help developers of all types are "tips and tools" blogs and articles. There is always a cleaner and more elegant way to do things when it comes to programming. Helping CFers to develop their best possible code can ensure that the CF stays alive. How so? If CF becomes too complicated to use, that will act as a deterrent to continuing with CF. Keep it simple when possible. Along with keeping code simple, tips on using certain tools and tags are important. These types of posts are great for education and keeping discussion open.

Finally, there needs to be community support. Allow for a group that caters to questions about CF and other IT related topics. Most CFers will keep things professional. But as the community grows the comfort level among individuals will also grow. This can lead to silly questions and topics. That is a good sign. Allow some of these topics to get posted as long as they are within an established set of community rules. Appointed moderators should regulate these feeds to maintain optimum relevance. But negative, name calling and character assassination need to be stopped in their tracks immediately.

Building and Strengthening the Community

A key concept to building the community is to encourage development. Motivation is a strong component to how well the community will perform as a whole. To motivate individuals, there should be a sense of structure in place. Elect administrators for the group. Choose people who are not only committed to building the community but themselves. These people can stand as pillars of inspiration to the rest of the community. The community and key members of should appoint evangelists. Evangelism is a very critical part of maintaining ColdFusion alive. The evangelists should be easy to talk to and knowledgeable about CF. Look for individuals with natural charisma and public speaking abilities. These people should strive to become the new face of ColdFusion. Excitement and enthusiasm are paramount to evangelism.

> *"I feel like ColdFusion really gives me a boost, especially being with it so many years that you know all the ins and outs, and even helping now with the open source versions in terms of the guts of it is great to see."*
> - Luis Majano President of Ortus Solutions

From CF Alive episode, "012 Extreme Testing and Slaying the Dragons of ORM with Luis Majano"

On the technical side of things, focus on two specific areas. Writing and Support. There are some members of the CF community who have a natural talent for writing. Not code, but actual text. Help these writers feel welcome and put them to work. A well-written blog can inform the masses and attract new prospects to the community. This can engage the community in all-important conversation. The writers should also work hand-in-hand with another group. The support techs. The techs should comprise of a group of expert CFers led by a seasoned veteran of troubleshooting (any names ring a bell?). These individuals should be able to provide support to those in need. Along with direct support, they should provide the writers with info to write about.

Another way to motivate developers is to remind them why they became developers in the first place. This responsibility should lie in the community itself. We should learn to motivate each other. Developers by nature crave challenge. The ability to create an operational platform out of nothing is rewarding. Remind the CF community why we do what we do. This could be a huge swing tactic when it comes to making sure the CF community remains happy and dedicated.

Finally, listen to constructive criticism and feedback. Don't only listen though. Embrace it. When a developer takes time to respond to something that means it has left a mark. That's a great sign. Encourage active engagement from the community. When the community responds, address the concern. Things cannot change overnight. But it is very encouraging to know that somebody is listening to your concerns. This can build trust among the CF community. Trust will keep CF alive.

Building and Writing Apps

One of the best ways to reach out to developers is to have them do what they do best. Build and write web apps using ColdFusion. Push for the development of new ColdFusion apps that are showcased to the public. Using and displaying applications built by ColdFusion demonstrates the usability of the platform. It allows others to see that ColdFusion is not dying. But it is still interesting and a viable language to use for development.

"Once corporations evolve and developers start getting into these workplaces, people need to start building apps."

- Luis Majano President of Ortus Solutions

From CF Alive episode, "012 Extreme Testing and Slaying the Dragons of ORM with Luis Majano"

Now that many apps don't expose the .CFM file extension, we need a "Built with CF" logo so that others can see what CF can do.

The next thing to do after creating these apps is to share them. Not only with other CFers (although that is pertinent to do), but with people outside of ColdFusion. Show them exactly what CF can do and how it can help with their programming needs. Through spreading of shared apps, CF is sure to make a resurgence amongst developers.

"I love the fact that I can be super productive in ColdFusion in a very short amount of time."

- Brian Klaas, Senior Technology Officer at the Johns Hopkins Bloomberg School of Public Health's Center for Teaching and Learning

From CF Alive episode, "037 Level Up Your ColdFusion Web Apps With Amazon Web Services, with Brian Klaas"

Write Modern Apps and Use Third-Party Applications

Don't stop at writing standard ColdFusion apps, write modern apps as well. What are modern apps? Modern apps are built using state-of-the-art development methods and tools. And are designed from the get go to be reliable, scalable, secure and easy to maintain.

> *"A lot of great experts that we share with that always seem to have an answer so I really just, relatively you know fast I see a lot of applications and in today's world I mean it's pretty hard to even create a slow ColdFusion page. I mean, you would really have to work hard at it to create a performance issue [because the CF server is so smart]. I've seen some really poor code and they still perform fine. These are pages that could take forever but still they work very fast."*

- Mike Collins,
Senior ColdFusion Consultant at <u>SupportObjective</u>

From CF Alive episode, "<u>062 Scaling Your ColdFusion Applications (Clusters, Containers and Load Tips) with Mike Collins</u>"

A big first step in writing more modern ColdFusion apps is through the use of Docker for containerization in the cloud. By packaging your existing apps into containers, legacy apps are given modern properties. This is done without having to change a single line of code. This process also improves app security, reliability, and portability.

Another great way of making your apps more accessible is to use CommandBox and ForgeBox. CommandBox functions as a package manager for your applications. You can use CommandBox functions to write and install code packages for you. This makes for a consistent and scriptable manner to install data libraries you need. After doing so, these packages may be uploaded and shared on ForgeBox. This will allow the entire CF community to start using them. Spreading applications keeps CF alive by making the app creation process simpler. Remember, sharing is caring.

Using third-party apps does more than improve the functionality of CF created applications. It demonstrates to the developer community the versatility of CFML. Most people outside the ColdFusion community tend to believe that CF is only for a niche group of uses. They couldn't be more wrong. CFML is one the most versatile programming languages available. Demonstrating versatility can bring more developers to the ColdFusion cause.

"We ask people is, how are you... what kind of apps do create... What are the reasons why you are still with ColdFusion? And one of things that we found out is 80% of the people believe that it continues to be to fastest development platform and delivers the maximum user features. And we do this every year. So it was 65% a few years ago, 70% last year, it's up to 80%. The next question that we would like to ask is, have you built any new applications with ColdFusion? And this year, the number was 78% of our folks are telling that they're building new applications. It's not just on maintenance. They are kind of going out and building new applications. And this is from 70% last year. So the trends are something that is really exciting more than the exact numbers."
- Tridib Roy Chowdhury, General Manager and Senior Director of Products at Adobe Systems

From CF Alive episode, "065 The Future of ColdFusion (it is Bright) with Tridib Roy Chowdhury"

For more details on these methods and other modern CF development approaches see chapter 1 Modernizing.

Community Engagement

An engaged, positive and supportive CF community makes CF more alive. In this section we look at different ways you can be part of the community, being more active and what we can do to make it better for everyone involved.

Be Part of the Community

"The new world in which we live needs new forms of cooperation."
- Peter Ivanov, Founder of <u>Virtual Power Teams</u>

From CF Alive episode, "<u>060 Virtual Power Teams for ColdFusion Development (3 mistakes to avoid) with Peter Ivanov</u>"

Most of you are already part of the CF community, but if you aren't.... JOIN! The CF Community needs your help. It is a great collection of great people. Yet, we need to bolster its ranks to keep moving forward in the future. There are few places to start your journey in that are worth mentioning.

- Join the CF Slack channel. This is a great place to ask and answer CFML questions. There are also sub-channels for CommandBox and other Box products, conference news and more.
- Join the CFML Facebook group.
- Update your LinkedIn profile with your latest CF projects and tool experience. Join the CF LinkedIn group. Make connections with other CFers. You will make new friends and it might led to a future CF job offer.
- Join the Adobe CF Community forums. Ask and answer CF questions or repost your CF blog content to share it more widely.

"If we're not engaging you in the right way or the way that you need to be engaged with, then let us know and we'll try to fix our processes. Get more help from the community in the way of blogs and techno articles on the community portal. Many times, our developers are very humble when it comes to the technology and the things that they've built and they are reluctant to share that information. Go outside of your comfort zone and share the solutions that you have and we'll all be better for it too."

- Elishia Dvorak, Technical Marketing Manager at <u>Adobe</u>

From CF Alive episode, "<u>030 Everything CF Summit That You Need to Know, with Elishia Dvorak</u>"

Be Active

"It's just an awesome language. If we forget my minor stint with PHP when I very first started development (which I think everyone did to an extent), ColdFusion is the first one that really took hold of me and I was able to understand. I think it's a brilliant language. I know that the rapid application development term gets bandied around a lot, but it's still very, very prevalent. I use other languages; I'll dive into Node, I dive into JavaScript. I played with Ruby, I played with Python. And they're all great for particular reasons. If you find a language that suits a task, use it. But I inevitably find myself coming back to ColdFusion because it does the job, and the language enhancements recently have been fantastic. If you look at the Lucee engine as well, I think it's opened up the gateway to a lot of ColdFusion developers. It's a very, very easy language to pick up. The community is one of the best still around. I think the ColdFusion community is amazing; always has been. I have made a lot of very, very good friends through that community, and it's kept me employed for quite some time. So, ColdFusion is a fantastic language. Plenty of people out there to help you. We want to see it continue to succeed because it is

succeeding. It's just a pretty language, so pick it up and use it if you haven't already."

\- Matt Gifford, Consultant Developer, <u>Monkeh Works</u>

From CF Alive episode, "<u>049 OAuth 2 for Me and You (Social Login Lowdown) with Matt Gifford</u>"

It's one thing to sign up, but the real advantages come when you get involved. Communities begin to thrive when each member does their part and contribute. You don't need to be super gung-ho but staying active is great. When members see your contributions, others are prone to emulate especially newer members. Be a role model for the community. Show others that it is OK to be active as well.

An added benefit of being active, is the network you can build while doing so. Put yourself out there and watch your CF potential grow.

Let this be the year that you stop lurking in online communities, only consuming and never contributing.

> *"My point is that there's a huge amount of people that are still using ColdFusion very happily. Sure there are some that have left, some that leave very noisily, some that leave grumpy and never want to look back, others who leave and say they're not coming back and then they end up coming back."*
>
> \- Charlie Arehart, Veteran server troubleshooter <u>CArehart.org</u>

From CF Alive episode, "<u>013 Are spiders eating your servers? The impact of their unexpected load and how to counter it with Charlie Arehart</u>"

Don't be a Negative Nancy

If we can say one thing about the development community, it's that developers love a good rant. Rants can be a good thing. They can show how passionate developers are about ColdFusion (and rightly so).

Just make sure to be respectful with your speech. There is no need for putdowns. Remember, you were starting out with ColdFusion yourself at some moment. How hard would it have been if you were put down for your lack of knowledge? Or if you entered a community full of unjust anger and hate? Keep positive and offer constructive criticism if needed.

> *"Less negativity. They've always surprise me that there are several members of our community that have threatened to leave over and over again that still keep coming back to just put the knife in as it were. Give it a bit of a twist to see if they can truly make the whole environment dead. I would just say little less negativity, and if people want to continue working with ColdFusion because they enjoy it, and they find it useful, will power to them. They should be encouraged to use it, and the community should be more about helping each other rather than denigrating various aspects of it."*
>
> - Geoff Bowers, Founder of <u>Daemon Internet Consultants</u>

From CF Alive episode, "<u>045 Secrets From the Folks Who Make the Official Lucee CFML Docker Images, with Geoff Bowers</u>"

There's an old saying that says, "There's always someone out there bigger than you." That applies to ColdFusion in a way as well. Nobody knows everything. If everybody knew everything, there would be no need for community. Be humble. Admit your shortcomings. Others will be more likely to assist you when you need it, as you should assist those in need as well. Share your knowledge with others so they can grow and strengthen as a developer. This, in turn, strengthens the community as a whole.

Again when you do help, keep rule number one in mind: Don't be a jerk. Offer help in a kind, professional manner. This helps to build rapport amongst the group and spur community involvement. It is very acceptable to comment on somebody's post. It is also acceptable to disagree. We all have differing opinions. But it is never acceptable to openly attack someone. As Yoda would say, "Hate is a path that leads to the Dark Side." The dark side in our case is the breakdown of community values and growth. And ultimately the death of ColdFusion.

To help us stay on the Light Side let's consider some possible community beliefs, values and guidelines.

What we hold true

ColdFusion is an alive and modern language. We are proud to use it. It is cool.

Together we can make it way more alive this year.

We believe in the magic that happens when intelligent developers create meaningful relationships and meet in person. We see the power of these connections to create better software and lives. Most importantly, we believe the difficult journey of software development is one better undertaken with others who can guide, inspire, and accompany you.

It's popular in the coding world to think that the point of developing software is simply to make money. Not here in the CF Community. We believe our businesses can be so much more too -- a path to personal freedom, legacy, a secure foundation for a family or community, or as a means for finding deeper meaning and abundance.

Our Community Guidelines

In the spirit of cooperation and communication, there's a handful of guidelines that help provide an environment where we can all learn and grow together.

They apply to the entire CF community. They apply everywhere you communicate with other CFers: in the forums, Slack, social media, at events, CF groups and masterminds.

- **Give more to your fellow developers than you ask from them (the CF imperative!); create more value than you capture.** Make your contributions in the spirit of helping the community. It's those who give that end up getting the most in return.
- **Operate with exceptional manners and professionalism.** Particularly when engaging in business deals with fellow members. Use explicit written agreements, contracts where necessary, and extend exceptional service to your fellow CFers. Be honest and upfront in your dealings, particularly when challenges arise (and they will!).
- **Be respectful and courteous with all your interactions.** Derogatory or insulting language is not tolerated.
- **Give your fellow CFers the benefit of the doubt or a 'beneficial reading.'** In many communities people make a sport out of picking apart the comments of others, here we seek to find the best in what others are contributing.
- **Prioritize shared experience over opinions.** Our membership represents some of the most remarkable doers, builders, and developers on the web-- we want to hear what you've done. CF discussions are at their best when we're sharing what we have done and what we have learned. You could call it talking your walk.
- **Don't have the answers? Welcome to the club. It's more productive to ask great questions.**

Our community values

- An abundant and giving mindset
- Honesty and directness in communication
- Service to our fellow developers
- Integrity
- Humility
- Thoughtfulness
- Cooperation
- Personal growth = developer growth
- Having fun!

How to Get the Most Out of the CF Community

There's many ways you can contribute and get value out of the community including:

- Host and attend meetups.
- Share a case study of something you learned in your coding.
- Share strategies, tactics and hacks that have worked well for you. Consider sharing a struggle you're having and collect suggestions from the community.
- Add value to other members' discussions by sharing your experiences in the forums.
- Join or start a mastermind for a specific CF area.
- Got an idea on how we can make the CF Community better? Email us. We'd love to hear it.

Keep Adobe Up-to-Date with Community Sentiments

As CF is very user-friendly to developers, Adobe is the same to the community. Some people don't realize this, but Adobe has an open-door policy. They also encourage developers and community leaders to use it. Write a friendly email addressing your concerns for CF and send it into them. Or post on the Adobe forum or bug tracker. They will read it. They have individuals dedicated to analyzing your input. For valid concerns, you will receive an answer from an actual Adobe representative. That is awesome! Adobe deserves more praise and recognition for this. Remember, they are part of our CF community.

On of the most effective ways to garner a response and start changes is to be thorough. There is always strength in numbers. Gather real quantifiable data and present your case. Present forth surveys and opinion from other members of the community. Express why your topic is a real concern. Adobe listens to its customer base. Now, it may take some time to respond. Some issues are not overnight fixes. Some need time to process and analyze to determine proper course of action. Learn to be patient. Hurried results are more often a bandaid, whereas proper response can be a permanent fix.

> *"I always walk away from these sessions inspired to be better, to go learn new things and to embrace the things that I've been exposed to. I walk away thinking there's 32 things I'm doing wrong at work right now and I need to go fix them."*

> - Scott Coldwell,
> Developer and Sysadmin at <u>Computer Know How</u>

From CF Alive episode, "<u>017 Managing an international team, Git, CFML, Node, Joomla, Headaches and Heartaches, with Scott Coldwell</u>"

Talk About CF in the Community

This seems like a moot point. But it does needs reiterating. A CF community should be talking about all aspects of ColdFusion. Most of the time, you will see members talking about issues and problems they encounter. That is fine. Addressing the issues is needed to usher proper fixes and changes. But sometimes it's nice to talk about the positives that ColdFusion has to offer. Everybody likes to see that their language is great and the strides it is making as a whole. Talk about the perks of using ColdFusion. Compare stories about how

CFML made their experience enjoyable. It is easy to learn and use. Highlight those points and bring positivity to the community. Make sure that the community knows that they are indeed part of something special.

> *"We got a lot of people building ColdFusion sites but we're just not real vocal about it. Maybe that's part of the shame that ColdFusion developers have."*
> - Gavin Pickin, Software Consultant for <u>Ortus Solutions, Corp</u>

From CF Alive episode, "<u>010 All things ContentBox (new API, ContentStore, Themes and more) with Gavin Pickin</u>"

Leading CF expert Charlie Arehart believes that CFers should take some initiative. They should become more aware of the resources available for ColdFusion. We can wholeheartedly agree on that. One of the best ways to do that is learning through the community. Members should also take the initiative and put that information out. It would help to motivate young developers into further pursuing ColdFusion. Also, take initiative not only on the forums but at conferences as well. Every speaker at conferences were once first-time speakers. If you have something valuable to contribute, get out there and do it. Volunteer to speak and help develop the community. This is an excellent way to help ColdFusion be more alive.

Let's Get Excited

Why isn't the community more exciting? Let's get pumped up over CF. There is a long-standing stereotype that developers are boring, uneventful people. We all know that this is not the case. Let's break that mold and show them what the community is made of.

"We're not making a big deal about it so most people think it's not there. They just assume it's something else. So maybe we should encourage people to say, 'Hey, this is built with ColdFusion'"

\- Gavin Pickin, Software Consultant for <u>Ortus Solutions, Corp</u>

From CF Alive episode, "<u>010 All things ContentBox (new API, ContentStore, Themes and more) with Gavin Pickin</u>"

What Would It Take to make the community more exciting?

Evangelism. A fresh new evangelist or team of evangelists is needed. Someone who can take the initiative and do it. Sure, anybody can give a brief powerpoint on features of ColdFusion. But what is needed is someone who can grab the bull by the horns. Someone to engage the public and community with gripping presentations. Get the audience involved. When giving live lectures, conduct activities that need audience involvement. Be humorous and witty. Get the crowd laughing. Let's make sure that each lecture or conference has that pizzazz that keeps you coming back for more. Online evangelism should be exciting and entertaining as well. Creating videos and skits related to ColdFusion could be a way to go. Developers are creators everyday with code. And creators are creative. So, let's spark that creativity and get the ball rolling.

> *"...it's just still a really fun product to work with. I mean I've been doing it pretty much my entire adult life as a developer. I certainly work with other products but it's still my first love kind of ... that I still really, really enjoy working with. We tend to get a lot of different clients that ... I'm able to really improve their websites, get them working better, getting them running a lot faster and error free. That just makes them happy about ColdFusion too, cause a lot of times they're being told that ColdFusion is the problem and we can show them that it's not the problem."*

- Mary Jo Sminkey, Senior Web Developer at CF WebTools

From CF Alive episode, "027 Advanced Error Handling Strategies for ColdFusion, Javascript and SQL with Mary Jo Sminkey"

Another way to get the community excited is to do something other than ColdFusion. Now, it sounds like it doesn't make sense but... Get active in the outside community! The community should get more active in sponsoring charity events. Hold pie-eating contests and take part in local or national fairs. Or sponsor a color run and participate as a group in events such as Relay for Life. The CF community doesn't have to be all about work. There are some good people in the community and potential good friends. Get some downtime in and be happier for it.

Conferences

Conferences are a wonderful way to get to know your community and learn about CF. Every year many CF conferences are held around the world bringing in CFers from all walks of life. Conferences can be fun and exciting as well. They embody the spirit of keeping CF alive.

"First thing is people. Whenever I go to a conference it's my opportunity to catch up with friends new and old. Also just to talk geek, talk shop, and I love that. We only have a limited number of developers in town here. I enjoy getting together with all of them whether they're mobile developers or Ruby developers or what-not. It's great to get together with all these ColdFusion developers and tell stories, share those war stories. There's a lot of smart people in the community and a lot of smart people are gonna be there. We've got a great number of speakers so I'm gonna enjoy that and having that time to be able to sit down and chat while you're eating.

I know it sounds funny but it's like people just sort of relax and you really get to connect with them a lot better and that's the thing about a conference. You get up early and you have breakfast with everybody and by the end of the night you're having a late dinner and just chatting around, everyone's got their computers out hacking or talking or whatever and it's just really good. It's just a great time with people."

- Gavin Pickin, Software Consultant for Ortus Solutions, Corp

From CF Alive episode, "010 All things ContentBox (new API, ContentStore, Themes and more) with Gavin Pickin"

Find Out What's New

As I stated earlier, conferences are great, especially when you get to attend. Keep up with the conference schedules. Make a calendar about when these conferences are happening. Mark them down and then share the good news. Help keep others in the community informed as well. A neat way to do this and make sure as many people as possible see it is to create a countdown. Create a countdown for your online groups. It's a fun and easy way to keep people up-to-date. You are also getting involved with the community which is a big win.

"I'm a big fan of the hallway track as a lot of people call it in conferences. I go to a lot of sessions. I also like to just talk to people in the hallway so I'll be at the Ortus booth and there will be a bunch of Lucee association members there as well and we're all looking forward to just talking with people. I get so many good ideas at conferences. I get a lot of feedback at conferences."

- Brad Wood,
Software Architect and Platform Evangelist Ortus Solutions

From CF Alive episode, "028 Design Patterns for amazing app architecture (16 patterns), with Brad Wood"

Attendance Tips

Here are some tips to help you be your best at conferences:

- Prepare and have a conference plan. Verify you have ample time to go to the conference. This includes downtime before and after the event. Conferences can be intense. You need to schedule recovery time.
- Tell clients and bosses up front that you will be off work for the whole conference time so that you can focus on improving your CF skills. There is nothing worse that attending a conference then spending the whole time in your hotel room tied to your laptop.
- Remember you don't have to attend every workshop. Meet up with a few individuals from your group and skip a lecture or two. Or make some new CF friends over coffee or a beer.
- If you have to travel far or overseas, plan your budget. Allow for snacks, drinks and unexpected expenses. That will make your experience less miserable than it has to be.
- If possible stay at the conference hotel. You will have many more opportunities to meet people at breakfast or in the elevators. Plus if you get knowledge overload and need a quick nap, your room is only minutes away.

Networking

"The schedule this year is insane. Luckily I'm only giving one talk so I can easily pop into the other tracks. But it's getting to that point now where I want to clone myself because there's something good in every

track. I'm primarily looking forward to actually catching up with a lot of friends and colleagues who I haven't seen for a while. Conferences are always an amazing place to do that; especially the CF conferences. It's kind of like a family reuniting once a year. To sit down, learn new stuff, catch up, and just be together."

— Matt Gifford, Consultant Developer, <u>Monkeh Works</u>

From CF Alive episode, "<u>049 OAuth 2 for Me and You (Social Login Lowdown) with Matt Gifford</u>"

Conferences are the greatest places to network in the CF community. Everyone attending is going to be a CFer or associated with ColdFusion. Talk with your fellow conference goers. If you have never networked before then just say "Hello, my name is ___". Often the other person was just as afraid to speak first and is glad you broke the ice. Then ask them about what they are doing with CF. They may have some insight into issues you may be having and can help you out.

"It's a great community of people and they're very friendly. It's a small group, so it's very intimate and you'll be able to really make great connections. There's some elements of fun about it that are unique to Into The Box and I'll just say if you're not coming then you're not going to know what you're missing, but if you come you're going to find out that there's a lot of fun. There's just a great spirit behind the conference."

— Charlie Arehart, Veteran server troubleshooter <u>CArehart.org</u>

From CF Alive episode, "<u>013 Are spiders eating your servers? The impact of their unexpected load and how to counter it with Charlie Arehart</u>"

There will be CF vendors and other third party tool companies present that can contribute to your CF success. Remember when you were a kid trading baseball cards? Now you can do the adult version and trade business cards! Collect as many business cards as you can and add these people to your network. They will be sure to do the same. Network with the speakers present. These individuals are often veterans and experts in the field. It is never a bad idea to have these people as friends.

> *"But when I sit down with them either a coffee or maybe over drinks at the event, then they start letting me know a little bit more about why that is. And I get the chance to really kind of interview them about how do they think it would make sense for us to move forward with that feature. What kind of things can we do? What are options in providing a solution for that particular problem?"*
>
> - Elishia Dvorak, Technical Marketing Manager at <u>Adobe</u>

From CF Alive episode, "<u>030 Everything CF Summit That You Need to Know, with Elishia Dvorak</u>"

Pro tip: Straight after you meet someone new at a CF conference, friend them on FB, LI or follow on Twitter. Even take a selfie with them and post that. This deeps your connection faster, is fun and when you need to chat with them in future months you are already connected.

> *"I'm primarily looking forward to actually catching up with a lot of friends and colleagues who I haven't seen for a while. Conferences are always an amazing place to do that; especially the CF conferences. It's kind of like a family reuniting once a year. To sit down, learn new stuff, catch up, and just be together."*
>
> -Matt Gifford, Consultant Developer, <u>Monkeh Works</u>

From CF Alive episode, "049 OAuth 2 for Me and You (Social Login Lowdown) with Matt Gifford"

Deep Learning

Conferences are also an enormous source of new material on ColdFusion. Many new updates to ColdFusion and other applications are released at conferences. Conferences are a wonderful place to share that information. A good trick to know is to bring a voice recording or video recording device. Record the most important speakers for you (only if permitted of course). This will allow you to playback and catch anything you may have missed the first time around. Also, this saves you from having to scribble down detailed notes so you can place your full attention on the speaker. The best part of gaining all this new knowledge is going back and sharing it with the community. Be sure to help those who did not have the good fortune to attend.

Apart from new material and updates, you can find out what's coming soon to CF at conferences. This gives you a chance to find out how these will affect your ColdFusion lifestyle. Keep track of what's coming up next by making a schedule and monitoring release dates. Again, share this information with the community. Spark conversation and get everyone excited over the incoming additions.

"I think one of the first steps is for people to attend conferences is to grow us developers and to learn things and to attend workshops like the CommandBox workshop just so they're always learning new things. One of the stark differences in a lot of other programming communities in ColdFusion is in a lot of communities people have a big focus on best practices and using the frameworks and using design patterns and using tooling. It's just baked in to the communities and expectation."

- Brad Wood,
Software Architect and Platform Evangelist Ortus Solutions

From CF Alive episode, "028 Design Patterns for amazing app architecture (16 patterns), with Brad Wood"

All in all, conferences are a great bang for your buck with everything that you learn from them. You may even score some free swag. Plus, the people that you meet and the connections that you build are invaluable. You will probably make new friends. If you are a first-time conference goer, it may be helpful for you to bring a friend from the community along with you. That could be someone you only know online until now. Conferences can be overwhelming for newcomers. Having a "conference buddy" may be what you need to have the best conference experience.

CF Summit

CF Summit is the biggest of all the ColdFusion conferences. This is definitely the place to be as a ColdFusion developer. Exchange ideas with CF developers from around the world. Learn new strategies to master your web app development skills. Who said CFers didn't know how to party? Speakers include the world's top CF experts such as Mike Brunt, Charlie Arehart and Brad Wood. And all the key Adobe managers and developers. Always talk with some of the speakers. Say hello, thank them for their presentation or ask questions. Remember to go to the conference with a goal in mind. Can't wait to see you there!

"I enjoy going and meeting with everybody that I haven't seen since the last conference or the last CF summit. And the reason why is that's where I get the most valuable conversations going, especially regarding feedback. I think a lot of times, people are less open to putting in a

detailed email with feedback that might take a long time to explain what they want and what things are bothering them about the CF."
\- Elishia Dvorak, Technical Marketing Manager at Adobe

From CF Alive episode, "030 Everything CF Summit That You Need to Know, with Elishia Dvorak"

Here's the list of all ColdFusion-related conferences that you should know about

1. Muracon
2. Adobe ColdFusion Government Summit
3. IntoTheBox
4. cf.Objective
5. NCDevCon
6. CFCamp
7. Adobe ColdFusion Summit
8. ColdFusion Summit East 2018

ColdFusion webinars

1. Ortus Developer Week
2. ColdFusion Docker Containers Roadshow Webinar
3. Adobe ColdFusion Developer Week

Related Article: A Comprehensive list of ColdFusion Conferences

Summary

- Stay educated on ColdFusion related changes and teach others.
- Reach out to new CF developers and inspire them to join the community.
- Get active in our CF community and give support to those in need.
- Attend conferences to learn, network and show our support for CF.

Let's look at how CF Marketing and PR could be improved in the next chapter.

CHAPTER 5

Marketing

"Transforming a brand into a socially responsible leader doesn't happen overnight by simply writing new marketing and advertising strategies. It takes effort to identify a vision that your customers will find credible and aligned with their values."

-Simon Mainwaring, Social Media Expert / Businessman

Without good marketing a product can die. There are some out there who say that Adobe ColdFusion is dying. Although ColdFusion experts and developers agree that it is very much alive. Perhaps the marketing of CF could be the problem...

What is marketing? "Promoting, advertising and selling." But marketing is much more than a simple textbook definition. It is a living system. It feeds and grows to fill its environment.

So what steps can we take as CFers to make sure ColdFusion doesn't fade away? How can we as users promote CFML?

These are some tricky questions as there is no clear-cut answer. Both producers and consumers must do their part to ensure survival of CF and help it grow. Let's take a look at how we can transform our quiet platform into a roaring giant through better marketing.

"Don't strive to be an 'expert' - stay hungry, be a student of your industry. Marketing is always evolving."

- Kirk Deis, CEO at <u>Treehouse 51</u>

From CF Alive episode, "<u>081 Better Bug Squashing (New Issue Tracking Tool) with Kirk Deis</u>"

Improve PR

"Welcome to The Greatest Show on Earth."

-P.T. Barnum, Circus promoter

Sometimes to find the best business tactics all we have to do is go to the circus. In the 1870s, one man reached out and touched history in both the circus and in the realm of business. Founder of Barnum and Bailey Circus, P.T. Barnum is considered to be one of the greatest PR reps in history. He was way ahead of his time when it came to promotion, sales, and closing the deal. Barnum understood what it meant to draw a crowd and get them excited for what was in store.

"ColdFusion from a technical point of view is not dying. What I believe is and has always been an issue in my opinion with CF is PR. Adobe has never really marketed ColdFusion to the masses and they've always been fortune 500, big corporation type clients they're going after, which doesn't get into schools and the mainstream. And Lucee has done a lot and for them to make it available to people who don't have big corporate checkbooks. But marketing has always been a weak point. I believe it needs more in the marketing department because the language is stable. It doesn't have any tech issues. It's got a good support base it just needs visibility."

- Steven Neiland, Senior web developer at <u>SiteVision Inc</u>

From CF Alive episode, "031 Going Modular With Fw/1 Subsystems 2.0, with Steven Neiland"

Unfortunately, we cannot say the same about the good folks at Adobe and Lucee. Apart from working CFML developers, very few know the name ColdFusion. Whereas, Java and C++ have become household names in tech circles. How can we do the same for ColdFusion? To do this, we must first address how CF's PR could be way better.

ColdFusion is far from dying. The advancements made in CF 2018 are amazing. Asynchronous programming, auto security lockdowns, and multi-latency support are some of the new updates. But let's be real, who is going to hear about it? It seems that this new content is going nowhere. The CF community needs to step up its game when it comes to getting the word out to the masses.

Adobe focuses its marketing to existing customers. It relies on word-of-mouth marketing more than wider outreach campaigns. The CF team also needs to reach out to their desired clientele. Adobe stays in its safe zone of Fortune 500 companies and government. Why aren't they reaching out to the developer masses? Why are they content to stay in this shell? New recruits keep a software army going. Notice how many ColdFusion experts are currently out there. The numbers are fewer than they could be. Also many existing CFers seem kind of ashamed about what they do, as I discussed in detail in the Introduction chapter.

Adobe ColdFusion isn't without its competitors in the CFML arena. The frontrunner of these is Lucee, an open source CFML. The Lucee Organization is currently not as prominent as Adobe in the public eye but rising. So why is it that Lucee is now mentioned in every conversation about CFML? First, Lucee as an organization is reaching out to the masses of developers. Lucee offers what Adobe does not - a free open source product.

But Lucee also offers some things that Adobe definitely could:

- A modern, streamlined community website. (Separate from the main corporate website).
- Partners that actively promote Lucee CFML, including the prolific third-party CF company Ortus Solutions.

What would help Adobe ColdFusion? Active marketing.

Instead of waiting for new customers to come to them, Adobe needs to reach out to new people. A safe place for them to start would be to expand within the Fortune 500 companies and government organizations they are already associated with. And then move beyond that to Russell 2000 and Inc 5000 companies.

We keep talking about marketing to the masses... but how to do that? Reach out to a younger audience. Target schools and universities and get fresh faces while they have not solidified their programming language "political views."

ColdFusion is an easy programming language to learn. All students interested in a software development path should be exposed to CFML.

Adobe currently has a program for student outreach with Adobe Education Exchange. But when was the last time you heard a public announcement about that? Instead of only handing out a free software to a student who can market to their institution, make a scene about it. Hold hackathons. Give out prizes to top school CF coders.

Related Article: Comprehensive list of Adobe ColdFusion learning resources

Let's Talk About Age and Its Benefits

"Being old doesn't necessarily mean you're not good. In fact, being old means that you're tried and true. The question is whether you're moving forward."

- Nathaniel Francis, Works at <u>Computer Know How</u>

From CF Alive episode, "<u>008 The Best REST You've ever Had: ColdBox REST with Nathaniel Francis</u>"

ColdFusion has been around since 1995. Back in the Allaire days, it was revolutionary. So much so that it has kept going over the last 23 years through the ownership by Macromedia and now Adobe.

"And don't believe the people who say, "Nobody uses it." Because I get new customers every week. I've got over a 1000 customers last 10 years. And they've run the gamut from small to huge to agencies to government to see universities and all kinds of segments in between."

- Charlie Arehart, Veteran server troubleshooter <u>CArehart.org</u>

From CF Alive episode, "<u>013 Are spiders eating your servers? The impact of their unexpected load and how to counter it with Charlie Arehart</u>"

ColdFusion has stamina. It has a unique tag-based language with powerful scripting. It is easy to use and easy to learn. It has lots of features built in that other languages have to use third party addons for. It is the glue between different systems and APIs.

"I think the first time I used ColdFusion was in my college days, and this was way back long time back. So I started using ColdFusion there. At that time, I realized how easy it was."

- Kishore Balakrishnan,
Senior Product Marketing Manager at Adobe

From CF Alive episode, "058 All about the Adobe CF Summit East 2018 ColdFusion with Kishore Balakrishnan"

It is tried and trusted.

It is the most secure web programming language according to a CNET analysis. And as I discussed in chapter 1 Modernize, it can be the most state-of-the-art web development ecosystem. Bar none.

"There is always something new out there. But, the question I ask myself is, am I able to accomplish everything with what I have and in an efficient manner. With ColdFusion the answer for me has always been Yes! Using ColdFusion I have built many applications for over 20 years, including the best e-commerce platform Slatwall Commerce, and it continues to be a technology that we can rely on."

- Sumit Verma,
Partner and Vice President at ten24 Digital Solutions

From CF Alive episode, "076 Slatwall ColdFusion eCommerce Unleashed (Beyond Shopping Carts) with Sumit Verma"

So why aren't we talking about it more?

Where's the buzz? This particular issue doesn't only lie on the backs of Adobe and Lucee. This applies to the CF community as a whole. **Stop being scared to bring up ColdFusion and CFML in larger IT communities.**

Believe in your development tools. Just because others aren't using it doesn't mean it isn't good or in many areas the best.

> *"I was one of the many web designers who boot-strapped into web development by learning ColdFusion in the late 90's. At the time was "HTML on steroids." Already familiar with tag based mark-up, it was relatively easy to learn the tag based coding -- at least the basics. But while we came to it for the ease of adoption and speed of development, we stayed with it for its power and reliability. ColdFusion is -- and continues to be -- a powerful, reliable, growing, cutting edge programing language."*

> - <u>Bouton Jones</u>,
> IT Business Systems Analyst Senior at Anonymous

From CF Alive episode, "<u>053 ColdFusion Practical Digital Accessibility (revealing 3 you didn't know) with Bouton Jones</u>"

Adobe ColdFusion is a great product. Developers have been using it successfully for decades. Be proud that you are part of a long standing community. Spread the good word throughout the realm of IT. Word of mouth marketing can be more powerful than a slick marketing brochure or ad.

> *"I think that Adobe can do a great job promoting ColdFusion. But I think that all of us who are in the ColdFusion community can make it that much better. And I think the other thing is you need to go out, and outreach to developers. I mean developers treat language like their*

religion, or their framework, or like a religion. So, you're not going to convert somebody who is hard core .Net or Java for example. That's a religion. But you can make the case to business customers about why using ColdFusion is a great choice."

           - Thomas Grobicki, CEO of <u>Avilar Technologies, Inc</u>

From CF Alive episode, "<u>041 The true ROI of ColdFusion (How to Sell CF to your Boss or Client) with Thomas Grobicki</u>"

Speaking of spreading the good word...

Evangelize CF

What the ColdFusion community needs now are more members like P.T. Barnum - a ringmaster with knowledge of the product and the tenacity to spread the message. A real spokesperson. Talking about ColdFusion is not enough, so let's shout about it! Before, Ben Forta was the evangelist for Adobe ColdFusion. That has since changed. He has taken to other projects alongside ColdFusion. His last blog update for ColdFusion was in September 2017. We thank Ben for everything he has done for ColdFusion. He has made a tremendous impact over decades.

Now, the evangelical side of Adobe ColdFusion is on a rapid decline. Other platforms have their own evangelists. People who are as recognizable as their product. Lucee has Gert Franz. Ortus Solutions with its Box products has Brad Wood, Luis Majano, Gavin Pickin and its module master Eric Peterson.

Who does Adobe ColdFusion have now? CF has many strong veteran developers and community leaders. Yet, we as a community need somebody to step up and take the mantle. Who will step up to be the face and champion of ColdFusion? A new fresh face for evangelism would be monumental in promoting CF.

"I would like to see something more from the CFML community as far as the providers, the software providers. We have other providers and I would like to see them be more prominent in what's going on. Ortus Solutions has been doing Into The Box. I would like to see other software developers take that sort of evangelistic approach to what they're doing as well, so that they're out there in front of people constantly. I think that's important to keep the community alive. Not just advertising, not just showing up at a conference with a booth to say this is my product, but take your product out and do a roadshow with it. I think that would make a big difference to people."

- Steven Hauer,
International Business Manager for <u>Bridges for Peace</u>

From CF Alive episode, "<u>021 Behind the Scenes at CFObjective, with Steven Hauer</u>"

Another thing to take note of is controversy. Controversy isn't always such a bad thing. P.T. Barnum said "There's no such thing as bad publicity." Let's find someone who can go out there and preach that CF is the best programming platform around. Someone who can stir the pot. Let's get Java developers talking about us. And PHP ones. And NodeJS. And CIOs. The more the ColdFusion name gets out there, the more people will come to check out the fuss. The amazing CF technology almost speaks for itself. It just needs a little help from some new evangelists.

#coldfusion

There are <u>2.62 billion</u> social media users worldwide, including Facebook, Twitter, LinkedIn, Instagram, Pinterest, Reddit and YouTube. Of the <u>21 million</u> developers of any language in the world, most are on some social media. You would think that some of these would be interested in CF. So where is ColdFusion?

Adobe ColdFusion's social media presence is underwhelming to say the least. The Facebook pages have relatively few posts, leaving you feeling unsatisfied. ColdFusion's twitter is also little-populated, tweeting on average of once a month. LinkedIn is pretty empty of ColdFusion posts. The hashtag searches for #ColdFusion and #CFML offer little more. Only a scant handful of individuals post with these hashtags. Even the ColdFusion Reddit, and the tech-focused Hacker News are close to empty.

Potential CF developers might ask themselves: "If Adobe doesn't care about putting up a nice front for their product, is it even that good?" Those who use ColdFusion know that it is internally, but hearing it from the manufactors regular helps keep CF alive in our minds.

Most companies now hire dedicated social media managers. Adobe even offers social media management platforms. So why is there no push for their own product? ColdFusion isn't dead. It's only hiding, and it's hiding right in front of our faces.

What Would It Take to Improve ColdFusion's Social Media?

This can be a simple fix. The real trick is to get the following of the youth. Get young developers involved. Younger people are 10x more likely to follow social media than older individuals. Remember, times change along with the generations. Today, younger developers are searching for what can give them the most excitement and reward out of life. ColdFusion's social media presence could support that with daily updates and news.

Another way to encourage young people is to make specialized groups for young CF developers. The admins for these groups should be active, veteran CF'ers. When budding developers have questions, they should be replied to with diligence. In the age of smartphones, checking your social media is easy. An active crowd always draws a crowd. (There's another trick from P.T.). This is already being accomplished in a way with the current private forums on

ColdFusion. Bring it to a more public forum.

Related Article: CFML Slack

Talk with CFers

"So, I just want to touch upon the reason why we're focusing so much on performance. What we've realized was based on the one on one conversations we've had with customers and also various road shows we've been having over the last couple of years. I realized that based on the conversations that 71 percent of our customers have goals associated with improving the performance of the application. You want to improve the end user response time, make sure that the service is available...They want ColdFusion service to be available to ensure that they can do business."

- Rakshith Naresh,
Senior product manager for ColdFusion at <u>Adobe</u>

From CF Alive episode, "<u>042 Revealing the ColdFusion 2018 Roadmap details, with Rakshith Naresh</u>"

Another way to market CF is to find out what the people actually want. Then give it to them.

Adobe CF Senior Product Manager Rakshith Naresh actually has a pretty ingenious way of doing this. When he goes to conferences and gathering for CF, he presents the attendees with a situation. He tells each of them to imagine they have a $100 dollar bill. This will be used for a simulated investment purpose. He next asks the crowd what they would like to see come out for ColdFusion. Afterwards, he arranges a list of potential investment prospects out. Rakshith goes on to ask each person where they will invest their $100 and in what amounts. So, one attendee may want to invest $75 in performance side issues and the other $25 in security issues. Another may want $30 in performance, $20 in security, and another $50 in real time customer support. At the end of this process, you can see where the people want their time and money invested in CF.

He does this all around the community and gathers data. This way of measurement actually helped with the release of ColdFusion 2018. But how can we reach beyond conference attendees to "9-to-5 CFers" and find out their needs?

> *"One of the things we need to do is measure what's making a difference. There is a decline at that point in the number of ColdFusion people who are publicly visible. I think that's actually true, because more and more of the ColdFusion jobs, like Ford Motor Company thrive on ColdFusion. They absolutely love it. There's a lot of other companies like that. They're selling more ColdFusion. You know where all the sales are going? Apparently the Wizard of Oz is the one who's buying ColdFusion, because it's all behind the curtain, it's places we can't see it."*

> - John Farrar, CEO, <u>SOSensible Group</u>

From CF Alive episode, "<u>018 VUE More With Less, with John Farrar</u>"

The answer goes back to social media and forums. Create simple three-question surveys for the CF community. The key to making these surveys work is to respond to the results. Make the results real-time so users can see what others think. Allow only a brief period of time -- say, one week -- before closing the survey. Then the admin of the group should communicate the results.

Ask the community then What Would It Take to make these things happen. In order for this to work, Adobe must be active in the group.

"Adobe has even said in a blog post last year that they were selling 2000 new licenses of ColdFusion 2016 per quarter. And people said, "Oh you mean updates or you mean upgrades or you mean maintenance subscription renewals, right?" And he said, "No, no, no, no, these are new people who've never had ColdFusion before buying it." That just flies in the face of the conventional wisdom that nobody's using ColdFusion anymore, it's a dead language, only government uses it. And it's just not true."

- Charlie Arehart, Veteran server troubleshooter CArehart.org

From CF Alive episode, "013 Are spiders eating your servers? The impact of their unexpected load and how to counter it with Charlie Arehart"

Rebrand

ColdFusion is not dead. It is very much alive and has been for over 20 years. This longevity can be contributed to many factors, but the fact still remains that some see it as old. Yet, it carries with it an air of complacency. There's an old adage that says, "If it ain't broke, don't fix it." Well, the problem with that saying is that it doesn't take account of changing views and markets. Adobe has to learn to grow with ever-changing views on software marketing. Follow the trends. Unfortunately, the trend is to state that ColdFusion is dying. So, how do we follow that trend without killing off our beloved platform? Well, maybe it's time to let it die.

Wait. What? Let it die? Well, yes but not exactly. Let's kill off the old way of thinking. Let's kill the trend itself by rebranding and marketing a new face of ColdFusion. This would not be the first time ColdFusion has been transformed.

- Allaire
  - o The original CF was named Allaire Cold Fusion 1.0. This type of naming system remained until November of 1998. The space was removed between "Cold" and "Fusion" to become "ColdFusion". The new spelling stuck and has been this way ever since.
- Macromedia
  - o After the acquisition by Macromedia, ColdFusion was again rebranded in May 2002. It was now Macromedia ColdFusion MX 6.0. Again, CF continued to exist as such until once more the product changed company hands.
- Adobe
  - o When Adobe acquired Macromedia (and hence ColdFusion) they dropped the "MX" and went back to just numbered versions. This started with Adobe ColdFusion 8. Then in 2016, Adobe gave the ColdFusion name a facelift. It dropped the version number and went with a year instead. We have now had Adobe ColdFusion 2016 and now CF 2018.

So, why the big fuss? Well, the majority of young developers are given the idea that ColdFusion is dying. What if we keep the great ColdFusion technology and let the CF name die or evolve? The younger generation now equates updates and new versions with images. Something other than numbers.

For example, what are Apple's new Mac OS versions?

- Sierra
- High Sierra
- Mojave

Or Android OS versions?

- Marshmallow
- Nougat
- Oreo

Would it be so bold if ColdFusion were to follow suit? This type of system could be beneficial in attracting the younger generation into CF.

During construction of new ColdFusion versions, production codenames are assigned. Previous production names include Centaur, Zeus, Splendor, Raijin and Aether. These names would appeal more to a younger generation over simple numbered versions. Particularly if they had a common pattern to them, like the sweets of Android or the California places of Apple.

The ColdFusion name has been dragged through the mud for a few years now. This becomes off-putting to those interested in entering the community. A fresh rebranding could be what is needed. This also would hit home to other developers (both CF and other languages) that ColdFusion was being refreshed.

Invest in your Workplace

Remember the USB 1.0? It was great all the way up to the point where it wasn't. It served its purpose well, but with the advent of USB 2.0 and micro-USB the original no longer had that pizzazz. Sure, it still functioned, but why would you keep it with the better alternative was available? The same thing can be said about ColdFusion. There are still many developers out there using ColdFusion 8 and 9. These systems are outdated by 10 years! 10 years in the computing world is two lifetimes. It is easy to see why some people stop using CF when they are using such old technology.

There is a simple solution. Upgrade to the current version of Adobe ColdFusion or switch to the current version of open source Lucee CFML

> *"They cannot be stuck in the CF8 or CF9 days. They have to invest in themselves. These corporations are doing tremendous amounts of money with ColdFusion, they need to evolve. They cannot stay where they are."*
> -Luis Majano, President of Ortus Solutions

From CF Alive episode, "012 Extreme Testing and Slaying the Dragons of ORM with Luis Majano"

Promoting New Versions of CF

Adobe does a good job of promoting each new release of CF to existing users. They have a two year release cycle. At the beginning they do a lot of surveys and interviews to find out which new features are needed.

What Would It Take to stay up to speed with the latest CF release?

The answer is easy. Invest in yourself and your work and update. What is it about updates that drive people away? Updates come with a plethora of benefits. They allow you to gain access to new features that can help you succeed in the world of ColdFusion.

In the ColdFusion 2018, for example, there is an auto lockdown feature. This saves you time (which in turn saves money). It allows for proper security measures to be taken with the click of a button.

There is no reason to get stuck behind. Updates are how your platform performs better, stays secure, and builds better applications. Modernize your work space. For optimal performance of ColdFusion, security tools, and other supporting systems, update! Keeping up to date software helps keep CF alive and modern.

Related Article: Adobe ColdFusion 2018; Step Into the Aether

Some CFers are reluctant to upgrade to the "dot zero" release of a new version of ColdFusion. Some new releases have had bugs in them.

(The MX 6.0 release was infamous for this issue). My advice is that if you are risk-averse then wait until the first hotfix has come out or 6 months - whichever comes first. It is then safer to upgrade. Of course you always want to test your code and app on a staging server with the new version to be sure everything still works the same way.

Hidden ColdFusion

There are many developers and companies that use ColdFusion in the open on public websites. They are proud to acknowledge their platform, and that is awesome.

But there are also many who use CF and hide the fact. For good security and SEO reasons URLs don't end with "CFM." The CF server is told to not broadcast ColdFusion and version info in the page header. This makes identifying that the website was built using ColdFusion difficult or impossible by sites such as BuiltWith.

> *"These days, I don't know if you noticed or not but everyone is like, "Oh, I found a site that's running ColdFusion." That's the site that has CFM still in the name. Still in the URL. But I don't know how many sites that we've built, but you don't ever see CFM in there. You never see the file extension. So, how many sites out there are ColdFusion that nobody even knows about?"*

- Gavin Pickin, Software Consultant for <u>Ortus Solutions, Corp</u>

From CF Alive episode, "<u>010 All things ContentBox (new API, ContentStore, Themes and more) with Gavin Pickin</u>"

Is there some secret society dedicated to keeping ColdFusion underground? Are these companies and developers ashamed to admit they are using it? If so, why? There is no need to hide your development platform. There are many more ColdFusion sites than are commonly noticed.

We need a "Built with ColdFusion" logo that you can put on such "hidden" sites, so that others can see what CF can do.

A great way to keep CF alive is to actually recognize the power of the platform. By using popularity as a tactic, ColdFusion is sure to garner more attention and in turn raise its user base.

> *"I like ColdFusion because I'm a consultant for a living, so clients will call me and say, "Here's what we want to build: some sort of mobile app or web app or what have you. What do you recommend we use to get the job done quickly, securely, write code that we can actually maintain moving forward?" I try to be as objective as I can with clients, and I look around and and think "Okay, what languages and tools are out there that would be the best solution for this client?" Nine times out of 10 it's ColdFusion. I get more done per line of code, out of the box, with a ColdFusion engine and code base, than I do any of the other similar options out there."*
>
> - Nolan Erck,
> Owner and Chief Consultant at <u>South of Shasta Consulting</u>

From CF Alive episode, "<u>005 Dependency Injection, why is it awesome and why should I care? with Nolan Erck</u>"

One way to get this in motion is to survey a sample all IT personnel and CIOs. CF companies and (apparently) non-CF ones. That would give us a better idea of the true market share of CF.

CF users could give us insight into why they are proud of it and what they want to improve about it. Also, interview non-CF users to determine why they are not using it. What is driving them away from ColdFusion? Do they not have personnel trained to use it? Or is the stigma of a "dying" platform scaring them away? Or is it something else? Adobe and Lucee should take these answers and address the biggest issues. Not everything has to be changed at once, but action does need to be taken.

Summary

This is What It Would Take to make CF marketing more Alive:

- Adobe ColdFusion marketing needs to do more outreach.
- Create a separate, modern website for ACF to showcase all it does and how the CF market is growing.
- Public relations campaigns from Adobe, Lucee and others in the CF community.
- A new CF evangelist(s) who has the audacity to challenge other languages.
- More CF social media and use of the hashtags #ColdFusion and #CFML. Hire a social media manager and have daily posts.
- More market research and surveys to show CFers that their opinion matters.
- Rebrand ColdFusion version naming to something more modern.
- Update to the latest version of ColdFusion.
- Unhide ColdFusion on your site

Next we look at how the CF Alive podcast got started and what is in the future for it.

CHAPTER 6

CF Alive Podcast Behind the Scenes

"There's only one interview technique that matters... Do your homework so you can listen to the answers and react to them and ask follow-ups. Do your homework, prepare."

- Jim Lehrer, American Journalist

When I interview CF experts on the CF Alive podcast, I definitely have to do my homework. To ask interesting questions. And I pay very close attention to their answers. Now, it's my turn to pay attention to the questions. Not to say that it's bad though. I love reaching out to members of the CF community and talking about the latest methods and trends in ColdFusion. I guess it is only fair that I answer some Frequently Asked Questions about myself and my direction in CF. Let's get started!

Background

Tell us more about yourself. How did you get into programming in general?

I was born in Berkshire, England in 1964. At a young age I realized I had a talent for mathematics and software development. I pursued my gifts and graduated from Cambridge University with a Bachelor's and Master's degree in Mathematics. And lots of side project experience in programming. From machine code, to assembler, to Basic. This was back in the 1970s and 80s. There was no web development or even Windows back then.

From there, I entered the rapidly changing world of software development and project management. I worked for a large UK software consulting company called Scion. Both in England and in Holland. I founded TeraTech in 1989 in Rockville, MD in the United States to build custom software and help others with their business problems. I have over 35 years experience with programming and project management.

Along with programming services, I teach Kundalini yoga and energy healing. I feel my calling is helping people grow and transform. For me, the yoga and IT work go hand in hand. The yoga gives me the balance to handle the stress of high-pressure IT projects.

With so many other programming languages, why ColdFusion?

By the early 1990s, TeraTech was focused primarily on Windows database programming using Visual Basic. However, my intuition told me that the future was in web programming.

When I had a client tell me of a project in a new web programming language called Allaire DBML (Database Markup Language), I saw this as my opportunity. DBML was soon renamed CFML and I attended the DCCFUG and MDCFUG meetings (ColdFusion User groups in Wasington DC and Maryland). I found the CF community to be very smart and welcoming.

After about a year, TeraTech took over the MDCFUG and started what would become CFUnited Conference. The rest is history.

The energy and excitement of ColdFusion users is what inspired me to shift TeraTech over to focus on ColdFusion services.

"I like to make sure we're always inviting other people to be a part of that because it gives you a lot more ownership and feeling of contribution in the community when you can say there's people out there using something I've written and everybody can do that."

-Brad Wood, Software Architect and Platform Evangelist Ortus Solutions

From CF Alive episode, "028 Design Patterns for amazing app architecture (16 patterns), with Brad Wood"

How the CF Alive podcast started

When did the rumors about ColdFusion dying actually start?

I first noticed the rumors forming back in 2001. This was during the Macromedia takeover of Allaire. The rumors quieted after the announcement that Macromedia was continuing ColdFusion.

Yet with the buggy release of ColdFusion MX 6 in June 2002, the rumors reared their ugly head again. At this point, TeraTech created the CFBugHunt.org website and started a public tracking system for bugs within CF MX. Again the rumors quieted down with time.

In April 2005, Adobe bought Macromedia for $3.4 Billion. Once again, the rumors of ColdFusion dying became active again.

Since then, the rumors resurface every few years or so. It seems that the common driver for these is fear of change.

How did you start the CF Alive revolution? What inspired you to do so?

In all reality, TeraTech has never had any problem finding CF developers and projects. For others, it was a different story. We sent out our annual survey, "The State of the CF Union", and the answers we received were shocking.

The biggest concern we received was that CF was dead/dying/legacy. That's what got me motivated. I wanted to help rebuild the state of ColdFusion and the community's perception of it. So, the CF Alive revolution was born.

When did you start the podcast and why?

In 2017, I decided that I needed to take action to counteract the CF dying beliefs and the CF Alive podcast was launched. The main goal of the podcast is to show that ColdFusion is still a modern, vibrant, and secure language.

At the time of creation, there were no active CF podcasts. I felt that a dedicated ColdFusion podcast would fill the need for developers between conferences. The podcast can also reach out to those developers who are unable to attend conferences. It seemed like the best way to reach the widest base of CFers with new techniques, tools and the message that CF is alive and modern.

At the same time, I thought that pointing out the most common problems and the best practices for how to deal with them would help CIOs. It could also reduce the stress they have. Since I interview ColdFusion experts on the podcast, we cover real-world CF issues and their solutions.

The podcast is also a way to promote conferences to new attendees and showcase conference speakers to CFers who can't attend the event.

Show Content

How do you get your topic ideas for the podcast?

I do a lot of interviews of speakers at CF conferences about the topic they are presenting on. This both promotes the conference, and the speaker and gets their ideas out to a wider audience. I spoke to the speakers at the first independent Into The Box conference prior to the event. In April, I was able to attend ITB and find out firsthand why ColdFusion was alive for them.

To this day, I still get most topics from conference speakers. In return, we promote the speaker to new CFers. It's a mutually beneficial relationship.

Some of the items spoken about are driven from outside sources. The mini-series I did, "The Women of Tech", was actually inspired by #MeToo social media movement. Along with, Sophie Eng had just released her manifesto, "Hear Us Roar". Everything just fell into place.

> *"Women are more social. So, maybe if you know a woman friend who's going to a conference maybe there some sort of an offering that you can provide to other women can join as well. The conference benefits from having more women attend."*
>
> - Sophia Eng,
> Senior Manager, Online Marketing at InVision App

From CF Alive episode, "034 Hear Us Roar: A Manifesto for Women and Minorities in Startup, Tech, and Business Communities with Sophia Eng"

You ask What Would It Take (WWIT) to make ColdFusion more alive each show. You also ask why each guest is proud to use CF. What is the main significance of this?

For too long, many CFers have been ashamed to say that they code in CF to other developers. This still puzzles me. ColdFusion is a wonderful, reliable and secure platform. There should be no need to feel alone or be ashamed.

I feel that it is very helpful to hear CF veterans and experts share why they are proud of their platform. The hope is that these statements will inspire my listeners to take pride in CF as well.

As for WWIT question, ColdFusion isn't just a platform. It's a living ecosystem with its own community. In order to change CF or make it more alive, the participation of the community is required. By asking WWIT, we can hear great thoughts and suggestions from community leaders. The inspiring answers from CF experts over 80 episodes of the podcast helped in creating this book.

How many podcasts have you produced? Which are your most memorable?

We have released 82 podcasts so far. The exciting news is that we are on track to break 100 this year. My most memorable ones were the "2018 CF roadmap" with Rakshith Naresh and "The Future of CF is Bright" with Tridib Roy Chowdhury. I loved asking two of Adobe's top ColdFusion managers some of the questions that all CFers want to know the answers to. And learning why ColdFusion is alive and growing from their point of view.

I always enjoy bringing Charlie Arehart on show. He always has some unique insight worth hearing. His episode on CF Spiders was amazing.

Also, I love having Luis Majano on. He's the CEO of Ortus Solutions and all things Box. And has a great take on making ColdFusion Modern.

Brad Wood has been a guest several times, both for his speaker topics and his insightful analysis on the State of the CF Union survey results.

Who is next? Who would you like to come on to the show?

I am always looking for new CF speakers, bloggers, regular CF CIOs, PM and developers to come on the show. It would be great to hear the input from more around the community.

For example, I interviewed Thomas Grobicki about the ROI (Return on Investment) of ColdFusion. He is a long-time CF'er who is very passionate about the language. He hasn't spoken at a conference yet, and I hope that will change. He really has some good stuff to share.

I am always happy to have back previous guests. It's great to catch up and find out what is new in the part of the CF world.

> *"The networking that we can do is my favorite part. A lot of smart people. I love to learn and there's a lot of people speaking on a lot of different topics. Excited to learn but honestly mostly the networking is a huge draw for me and being able to rub shoulders with some of the great friends and great co-developers."*
>
> - Seth Engen, Co-owner of Computer Know How

From CF Alive episode, "016 Adventures with ColdFusion and ContentBox in the Wild, with Seth Engen"

Do you have any plans to do more outreach to the Lucee organization?

Absolutely. I talk with them regularly and love hearing about the strides Lucee is making. The open source version of ColdFusion is doing wonderfully. Helping the Lucee organization get more exposure is great for the future of all CFML.

Any future plans for conferences? Sounds like maybe you should speak or set up a booth. Does this seem feasible in the future?

I love going to conferences. I have presented at about 50 over the years. I fell in love with CF conference from the very beginning of CFUnited. We are planning to go to CFCamp again later this year. We had an outstanding experience at CFCamp in Munich last year. There were over 20 speakers including Mark Drew and Gert Franz. Lucee even sponsored the event which was great to see. I am really looking forward to what the 2018 CFCamp holds in store.

Also, I will be attending the CFSummit in Las Vegas. That event is sure to draw a crowd and be amazing. I am very excited for this year's conference season.

> *"When I went to my first conference three years ago I was still incredibly green. I was welcomed into the ColdFusion community with open arms and an overwhelming wave of encouragement. It's lead me to life long friendships and a dedication to learning as well as educating my development peers."*
>
> - Jeffrey Kunkel, Web Developer at Lighting New York

From CF Alive episode, "072 Oh my GAD (General Anxiety Disorder) with Jeffrey Kunkel"

The CF Alive Revolution

How do you plan to keep the CF Alive revolution going? Any plans to take it bigger?

The CF Alive movement growing. The podcast downloads have increased 600% over the last year. Here are a few ways I plan on continuing and growing the movement:

- This book
- Regular CF articles on the TeraTech website
- The CF Alive Podcast (my goal is to break 100 episodes this year)
- Webinars

My ultimate goal is that all CFers embrace the CF Alive revolution. Together, we can create a vibrant and modern CF.

> *"For it to continue I would just like to see more open source contributions. If we can keep the package management libraries populated with valid ColdFusion packages, keep the communications going, keep the chats going, keep the blog posts going, keep podcasts going... as long as we keep the buzz going, then I think it will continue to thrive."*

- Matt Gifford, Consultant Developer, <u>Monkeh Works</u>

From CF Alive episode, "<u>049 OAuth 2 for Me and You (Social Login Lowdown) with Matt Gifford</u>"

Finally, why are you proud to use ColdFusion and to be a part of the CF community?

The ease of coding and power of ColdFusion is second to none. It is reliable to produce secure and scalable applications. And do it fast. Both rapid code creation and apps that run fast.

With new supporting developments such as Docker's containerization, microservices and CommandBox, ColdFusion is a modern state-of-the-art development platform.

As far as the community goes, you would be hard pressed to find a greater group of people. ColdFusion would be nothing without the community behind it. I am proud to be a part of it.

Together, we can accomplish great things with CF and make it more alive this year!

CHAPTER 7

The CF Alive Reward

The CF Wanted Poster

Remember that CF Wanted poster from the Introduction Chapter? That ColdFusion is "Wanted, Dead or Alive" and there is a reward out for it. In this chapter I look at the reward you can get for finding CF Alive in more detail.

As I have shown in the earlier chapters, CF is thriving and is now the most modern and secure web development ecosystem.

My vision is that:

> We are confidently coding easy to maintain apps in CF. Enlivened by using a tried and trusted language. Unleashing the full efficiency of using ColdFusion in our work. We inspire other developers and young programmers to explore the power of CF.

Let's look at some of the remaining blocks to this and your reward if you overcome them.

Language Shame

ColdFusion is sometimes considered less cool and less "sexy" to code in, unlike some other newer languages or even the languages that are a similar age to CF such as PHP and Java. Developers often have a shame-y tone when talking about CFML. It is one of the main reasons for the CF's dying threads. This is a roadblock for re-establishing CF as a leader.

Once more CFers are proud of using and sharing their achievements with CF on blogs and social media, this will improve. By evangelizing what you have created in CF and publishing packages on ForgeBox or GitHub, CFML will also become more popular. It is wrong to think that one should be just humble and do your thing without self- promoting and standing up for CF when it is questioned. You're promoting not just yourself but also advocating for CF, and thus making sure ColdFusion stays alive.

> *"I'm proud to use ColdFusion. I've built a successful company on ColdFusion...the bottom line is that ColdFusion enabled me to build an application that sells, and sells well. I built other companies on other languages, and those companies no longer exist. So if you judge success by who brought you there, ColdFusion brought me here."*
>
> - Thomas Grobicki, CEO of <u>Avilar Technologies, Inc</u>

From CF Alive episode, "<u>041 The true ROI of ColdFusion (How to Sell CF to your Boss or Client) with Thomas Grobicki</u>"

For too long we have avoided sharing the cool projects we are working on with other developers. For years we have been stuck using old and insecure versions of CF, not feeling heard by our bosses about upgrading to new versions. Stuck in our CF skills, falling further and further behind the cutting edge. Worried about career opportunities, salary stuck due to working on CF legacy apps, staying in the same position for years on end.

My vision for the future of CF Alive is that we are no longer alone and ashamed coding in ColdFusion

No longer Alone in Legacy CF coding

Sometimes CFers have felt alone doing legacy CF coding; that they are not part of a supportive community. That even their bosses don't hear our challenges about using old versions of CF or old development techniques. There is never enough time or budget for training or doing things right. But always enough time to do it over or band-aid bug fixes.

So we keep slogging along with old-fashioned CFML. We can't give up, too near to retirement for that. Even though we can't see light at the end of the tunnel. Yet.

We have been afraid that we are stuck on the "CF Titanic". That it is slowly sinking... and it is too late to get in a lifeboat (to the supposed safety of "a different 'cool' language"). We lack the time and resources to build that lifeboat on our own. That CFML is no longer seen as cool and the computer press doesn't care about it.

Our worst enemy has been our own negative mindset about CF dying and legacy paralysis.

CF Legacy paralysis

Some CFers have "legacy ColdFusion fatigue". Perhaps they are avoiding learning new tools and methods, afraid to even try. How can we be re-invigorated learning modern CF methods and features?. Let's find again the excitement CFML coding and feel that it is "cool" once more.

Every year they have hoped that someone else will improve CF. But things just seem to get worse. So they just knuckle down and keep working on legacy CF maintenance.

Depressed about ColdFusion is Dead threads. Apathy from flame wars in CF community and haters who left but keeping coming back to snipe.

When CF first started with Allaire it was exciting, the cutting edge of web development. We used to feel that we had a voice and mattered and could influence the direction of CF. Now everything is corporate and slow moving. I know that people in Adobe are trying to change this and improve this. WWIT for this to happen sooner? (* WWIT = What Would It Take)

That decisions about CF are made further and further away from us. *They* don't listen. We as a CF community are constantly working on improving the CF and I believe that by working together with Adobe and Lucee, this might be a lot easier, faster and more efficient.

We have had enough risk avoidance and playing it safe. We are not afraid of rocking the corporate boat in order to reach the promised land of CF Alive. We have overcome thinking that every new programming language is the cool kid on the block, kicking dirt in the face of CF.

We brush Fake FUD (Fear Uncertainty Doubt) from other software manufactures off our shoulders.

Your Reward

What is the reward if you capture modern CF from that Wanted poster? '

Imagine your software engineering team was just 10% more efficient using modern CF. What kind of business results would that drive? Can you quantify it?

Here are more questions to get you the rewards of modern CF Alive:

- What Would It Take (WWIT) to get 10% better results with modern ColdFusion this month?
- WWIT to get started with modern CF today?
- WWIT to try out a new CF tool this week?
- WWIT to make your CF code and server more secure?
- WWIT to make CF more alive this year?

Join the CF Alive revolution

Now that you have read this book and seen all the ways that ColdFusion is alive, modern and secure I invite you to join the CF Alive revolution.

There are several ways you can do this:

- Become an advocate for CF in your company and local developer community
- Attendee CF conference and webinars'
- Listen to the CF Alive podcast and be interviewed on it
- Write inspiring blog posts about your CF experience
- Step up in the CF community, help other CFers
- Become a leader that helps grow this venture far beyond ourselves.

Let's all make CF more alive, modern and secure this year!

APPENDIX A

The Interviewees

Thanks to all the CF experts who were interviewed on the CF Alive podcast and were the inspiration for this book.

Alex Skinner

Alex Skinner is the managing director and co-founder of global digital agency Pixl8 (https://www.pixl8.co.uk/). Started with CF 4. Providing strategic direction and consulting on the more advanced projects undertaken. In addition, he works with our platform team to deliver our Open Source CMS and MVC Framework Preside CMS (https://presidecms-slack.herokuapp.com/).

Links:

- Preside https://www.preside.org/
- Preside CMS https://presidecms-slack.herokuapp.com/
- Twitter PresideCMS http://www.twitter.com/@presidecms

- Twitter Alex http://www.twitter.com/@meta_alex
- Twitter Pixl8 http://www.twitter.com/@pixl8
- Pix8l https://www.pixl8.co.uk/

Episode:

- 019 A Whirlwind Tour of Preside Application Framework in the Wild, with Alex Skinner

April Graves

April Graves is a Senior Software Engineer with nearly two decades of experience designing and developing software solutions for customers like the DOD, Public Safety, Financial Services and NASA. She has founded user groups, written for journals, presented at conferences, and currently a member of the NASA Speaker Bureau. April has used her education and experience to share knowledge with the new generation of Computer Scientists as a mentor and Adjunct Professor.

Link:

- LinkedIn https://www.linkedin.com/in/aprilegraves/

Episode:

- 036 Getting Real with Women in Tech with April Graves

Bouton Jones

IT Business Systems Analyst Senior at Anonymous

Links:

- LinkedIn https://www.linkedin.com/in/boutonjones/

Episode:

- 053 ColdFusion Practical Digital Accessibility (revealing 3 you didn't know) with Bouton Jones

Brad Wood

Brad grew up in southern Missouri and after high school majored in Computer Science with a music minor at MidAmerica Nazarene University (Olathe, KS). Today he lives in Kansas City with his wife and three girls. Brad enjoys all sorts of international food and the great outdoors.

Brad has been programming ColdFusion since 2001 and has used every version of CF since 4.5. He first fell in love with ColdFusion as a way to easily connect a database to his website for dynamic pages. He enjoys configuring and performance tuning high-availability Windows and Linux ColdFusion environments as well as SQL Server. Brad is the ColdBox Platform developer advocate at Ortus Solutions (https://www.ortussolutions.com/) and lead developer of the CommandBox CLI.

Links:

- CFML Slack Box Channel https://cfml.slack.com/
- Twitter https://twitter.com/bdw429s
- Brad http://www.codersrevolution.com/

Episodes:

- 002 First Look into the IntoTheBox Conference with Brad, Luis & Gavin
- 029 Design Patterns for amazing app architecture (16 patterns), with Brad Wood
- 070 CommandBox 4 Deep Dive (new version revealed) with Brad Wood

Bret Fisher

For 25 years Bret has built and operated distributed systems as a Sysadmin and helped over 30,000 people learn dev and ops topics. He is a Docker Captain, the author of the wildly popular Docker Mastery series on Udemy, and also provides DevOps style consulting and live workshops with a focus on immutable infrastructures, containers, and orchestration. Bret's an occasional shell and web, and JavaScript developer. He spends his free time in Virginia's local, thriving tech scene helping lead local Code for America and Docker Meetups. Bret basically spends his days helping people, and giving high fives. He lives at the beach, writes at bretfisher.com, prefers dogs over cats, and tweets at @bretfisher.

Links:

- Bretfisher.com http://www.bretfisher.com/
- Twitter https://twitter.com/BretFisher
- GitHub https://github.com/BretFisher

Episode:

- 066 The Docker Revolution for Faster ColdFusion Development (and Easier DevOps) with Bret Fisher

Brian Klaas

Brian Klaas is the Senior Technology Officer at the Johns Hopkins Bloomberg School of Public Health's Center for Teaching and Learning. As the architect for eLearning technology at the School, he leads a team that designs and delivers custom online courseware to students and members of the public health workforce around the globe. In addition to designing software and delivering courses, Brian is the manager of the Johns Hopkins Web Technology Forum, teaches "Introduction to Online Learning," and leads faculty training and development courses. Brian has presented on software development and eLearning at conferences throughout the country, including jQuery US (https://jqueryui.com/),

cf.Objective() (http://www.cfobjective.com/),
CF Summit (https://cfsummit.adobeevents.com/),
Into the Box (https://www.intothebox.org/),
NCDevCon (http://ncdevcon.com/),
Adobe MAX (https://max.adobe.com/),|
UBTech (https://www.ubtechconference.com/),
and CUE (http://www.cue.org/).

Links:

- Website http://www.iterateme.com/
- Twitter https://twitter.com/brian_klaas
- GitHub https://github.com/brianklaas

Episode:

- 037 Level Up Your ColdFusion Web Apps With Amazon Web Services, with Brian Klaas

Brian Sappey

Brian Sappey is an Applications Architect and Manager of Engineering. His most recent focus has been redesigning the E-commerce infrastructure at Market America/SHOP.com. He is an avid supporter and user of the Adobe API Manager.

Link:

- CF Summit Adobe Events
  https://cfsummit.adobeevents.com/agenda/

Episode:

- 054 How to implement Adobe's API Manager (with Swagger, ColdFusion, and API's) with Brian Sappey

Carol Hamilton

Carol is the cf.Objective (http://www.cfobjective.com/) Co-chairperson content advisory board and steering committee. She helps pick the venue, does marketing, advertising, and has been meeting every week for nearly a year to make the conference the best one yet. When she is not busy on the conference she is a super mom and developer.

Link:

- Twitter https://twitter.com/k_roll242

Episode:

- 028 Behind the Scenes at cfObjective, with Carol Hamilton

Charlie Arehart

A veteran server troubleshooter who's worked in enterprise IT for more than three decades, Charlie Arehart is a longtime community contributor who as an independent consultant provides short-term, remote, on-demand troubleshooting/tuning assistance for organizations of all sizes and experience levels.

Links:

- Twitter https://twitter.com/carehart
- Facebook https://www.facebook.com/carehart
- LinkedIn https://www.linkedin.com/in/carehart
- Web http://carehart.org/
- Consulting http://carehart.org/consulting

Episodes:

- 013 <u>Are Spiders Eating Your Servers? The Impact of Their Unexpected Load and How to Counter It, with Charlie Arehart</u>
- 032 <u>The Impact Of Unexpected Load and How To Counter It with Charlie Arehart</u>
- 033 <u>What's New In CF 10, 11, And 2016 That You May Have Missed? with Charlie Arehart</u>
- 067 <u>More you missed from Adobe ColdFusion 10, 11, And 2016 with Charlie Arehart</u>

Christine Ballisty

With almost 10 years of project management experience at the enterprise-level, Christine Ballisty has a wealth of expertise and understanding in effectively conceiving and executing complex software application and web development solutions. Christine has a successful track record of positive feedback from clients, key partners and colleagues with a proven ability to single-handedly manage a pool of onsite & remote Application Developers & User Interface Designers.

As she frequently manages several projects simultaneously, Christine also oversees budgets and cares for project lifecycles in an experienced, proficient and meticulous manner; all in tandem with leading the Project Management Office of Blue River. She currently provides oversight and guidance to a number of project managers and coordinators in the Professional Services division.

Links:

- LinkedIn https://www.linkedin.com/in/christineballisty/
- Twitter https://twitter.com/cballisty
- Instagram https://www.instagram.com/christineballisty/
- Personal Travel Blog http://christineballisty.com/

Episode:

- 079 Help Your ColdFusion Team Find Flow (7 keys to PM success) with Christine Ballisty

David Tattersall

David Tattersall has been in working in IT for over 30 years. Since co-founding Intergral (https://www.intergral.com/) in 1998, he focused on company management, business development and sales & marketing. Intergral has become a leader in server monitoring and application performance monitoring (APM) solutions in the ColdFusion / Java segment. His flagship product – FusionReactor – (http://www.fusion-reactor.com/) is used on over 25,000 production servers and has been purchased by over 5,000 customers.

Links:

- FusionReactor http://www.fusion-reactor.com/
- LinkedIn https://www.linkedin.com/in/davidtattersall/
- Intergral https://www.intergral.com/

Episodes:

- 006 CF State of Union Survey 2017 with David Tattersall
- 022 FusionReactor Application Performance Monitor – Why It's Different Than Other APM Tools and What's New in Version 7 & the CLOUD, with David Tattersall
- 046 What is new in Fusion Reactor 7 (20 new features), with David Tattersall

Dominic Watson

Dominic Watson trained as a Musical Theatre actor before embarking on a career in London's west end. Fortunately, this folly was cut short by an overtaking love of all things programming that led to a decisive career change building web applications.

Programming CFML for over 10 years, he is now the technical lead at Pixl8 Interactive (https://www.pixl8.co.uk/) , a London-based digital agency specializing in Web and Intranet development, and lead developer of Preside, our open source CFML CMS and application development platform.

Links:

- Preside http://preside.org/
- LinkedIn https://www.linkedin.com/in/dominic-watson-50770718/

Episode:

- 007 Marketing Automation using the Preside Platform with Dominic Watson

Ed Bartram

Ed has been a ColdFusion developer since 2000, first using version 4.5. He is currently co-manager of the Chicagoland CFUG (http://www.ccfug.org/) and previously co-managed the Nebraska CFUG in Omaha. While he has not spoken at a conference before, he has given several presentations to both groups. Ed has been a regular attendee of many conferences over the years including
Devcon (https://devcon.ph/),
Max (https://max.adobe.com/),
bFusion (https://github.com/bFusion),
CFObjective (http://www.cfobjective.com/),
Into The Box (https://www.intothebox.org/),
and CF Summit (https://cfsummit.adobeevents.com/). When he's not slinging code he likes to camp, hike, and work on his 1973 VW Beetle.

Links:

- Twitter https://twitter.com/@edbartram
- Ed Bartam website http://edbartram.com/

Episode:

- 080 Assert Control Over Your Legacy Applications (TestBox Quick Start) with Ed Bartram

Elishia Dvorak

Elishia Dvorak Technical marketing manager for ColdFusion. She started out as a CF developer.

Links:

- CFSummit https://cfsummit.adobeevents.com/
- LinkedIn https://www.linkedin.com/in/elishdvorak/
- Twitter https://twitter.com/elishdvorak
- Adobe blogs http://blogs.coldfusion.com/

Episode:

- 030 Everything CF Summit That You Need to Know, with Elishia Dvorak

Elliotte Bowerman

Elliotte Bowerman, is the Unicorn Muse and cofounder of the Unicorn Scouts (http://www.unicornscouts.com/).

Elliotte Bowerman, the Unicorn Muse, helps professional unicorns – women in tech – "get in their glitter" to get more pay, more power and more play in their careers and their lives. An award-winning journalist, tech PR executive and former VP of Marketing, Elliotte has worked with 20+ startups over the past dozen years. She's been the most senior woman at multiple tech companies, built and managed teams in difficult work environments, and learned how to bend and break "the rules" to turn her job into a lifestyle delivery system.

Elliotte is a single mother, soul marketer, entrepreneur, professional play-grounding guide, conscious life crafter, speaker, writer, workshop leader, artist, and magic maker. In addition to working with adults, Elliotte is also dedicated to helping "unicorn kids" – the magical ones that don't quite fit in with the herd – be seen, supported and encouraged to shine. In 2017, Elliotte co-founded the Unicorn Scouts with her 7-year-old daughter. She Kickstarted more than $10,000 to create a global community – a Glitter Guild – that brings artful, in-powering, magical odysseys to alternative folks of all ages. These adventures teach life skills – including shame resilience, creative self-expression, boundary setting, gratitude, mindfulness, and community – through interactive stories and playful missions delivered via physical mail + digital channels. A portion of all Unicorn Scouts and Glitter Guild proceeds go to support free outreach activities and sponsored memberships for at-risk youth.

Links:

- Unicorn Scouts http://www.unicornscouts.com/
- Facebook https://www.facebook.com/UnicornScouts
- Instagram https://www.instagram.com/unicornmuse/
- Twitter https://twitter.com/UnicornScouts
- Medium https://medium.com/@UnicornScouts

Episode:

- 040 The Opportunities of Being a Woman in Tech Today with Elliotte Bowerman

Eric Peterson

Eric Peterson is a CFML and Javascript developer at O.C. Tanner (https://www.octanner.com/) in Salt Lake City, Utah and more recently with Ortus Solutions (https://www.ortussolutions.com/) (ColdBox (https://www.coldbox.org/),
CommandBox
(https://www.ortussolutions.com/products/commandbox), etc.).

He attended the University of Utah and received a degree in Information Systems thinking he would hate programming as a career. He started programming in CFML (and in general) in 2012 and has never been more happy to be proved wrong. He is the current maintainer of ColdBox Elixir
(https://coldbox-elixir.ortusbooks.com/)
and a prolific module author on ForgeBox.io (https://forgebox.io/). He loves creating tools to help bring CFML up to date with other modern languages and communities. In his free time, Eric loves to participate in theater, musicals, and to spend time with his wife and two boys. He can be found on Twitter, GitHub (https://github.com/), and on his blog (http://dev.elpete.com/).

Links:

- Website http://dev.elpete.com/
- Twitter https://twitter.com/_elpete

Episode:

- 023 Modules Make Your Projects Have Superpowers, with Eric Peterson

Esmeralda Acevedo

Esmeralda Acevedo is a Software Consultant for Ortus Solutions, Corp (https://www.ortussolutions.com/). Her professional journey began about 17 years ago as a graphic/web designer, in the time of tables and frames. After graduating from California State University with a major in Art and a minor in Computer Science, she was hired to work along CFML developers. Although Esmeralda was mainly involved in the design aspect of the projects, she gradually became more involved in assisting the programming team.

Eventually, Esmeralda returned to school to complete a technical degree, with an emphasis on software development. Now, in addition to her experience with graphic design tools, such as Photoshop, Illustrator, Fireworks, Indesign, etc., she has added application development tools, which include CFML, MySQL, Javascript, CSS, Bootstrap, Coldfusion, Coldbox, ContentBox to the list.

Links:

- Ortus Solutions https://www.ortussolutions.com/

Episode:

- 015Better ContentBox Themes and Easily Creating an Amazing UI, with Esmeralda Acevedo

Gavin Pickin

Gavin Pickin – Software Consultant for Ortus Solutions (https://www.ortussolutions.com/).

Gavin started using ColdFusion in 1999 when working for the university of Auckland in New Zealand before moving to California. He has lead teams, trained new developers and worked the full stack from graphic design, HTML CSS JavaScript through to ColdFusion MySQL and server administration.

Gavin has a passion for learning and cannot understand why the 9-5ers aren't listening to podcasts while changing diapers, watching video tutorials while cleaning baby bottles and folding clothes, or putting the kids to sleep with soothing phonegap mobile application cookbook recipes.

Links:

- Twitter https://twitter.com/gpickin
- Website http://gavinpickin.com/

Episodes:

- 002 First Look into the IntoTheBox Conference with Brad, Luis & Gavin
- 010 All things ContentBox (new API, ContentStore, Themes and more) with Gavin Pickin
- 071 ContentBox in the Cloud (Docker Magic) with Gavin Pickin

Geoff Bowers

Geoff Bowers is a CEO of Daemon (http://labs.daemon.com.au/) in Sydney Australia for 22 years so far and a President of Lucee Association (LAS) (http://lucee.org/). He has ran WebDU conference (http://www.daemon.com.au/case-study/webdu-developer-conference) for 10 years.

Links:

- Website http://labs.daemon.com.au/
- Twitter https://twitter.com/modius

Episode:

- 045 Secrets From the Folks Who Make the Official Lucee CFML Docker Images, with Geoff Bowers

George Murphy

George is a long time CF developer, focused on ColdBox (https://www.coldbox.org/) and CF server maintenance. Currently

Senior Software Developer at Fig Leaf Software (https://www.figleaf.com/). He's been working with and exploring various web technologies since the late nineties. ColdFusion aficionado since version 4.5. ColdBox Evangelist. Loves collaborating with other developers and bouncing ideas off them and having them bounce ideas off me. I truly love spending and sharing my time with my lovely wife, daughter and friends.

Links:

- Twitter https://twitter.com/murpg
- Website http://www.websbygeorge.com/

Episode:

- 026 Gitlab Server Deep Dive with Continuous Integration, with George Murphy

Gert Franz

Gert was born in 1967 and lives in Switzerland since 1997. He is one of the key people behind Lucee (http://lucee.org/). Back in the late eighties he studied Astrophysics in Munich but switched to later IT as a profession and programmed for several companies in the past as a database administrator and system analyst.

Links:

- Rasia http://rasia.ch/
- Twitter https://twitter.com/gert_rasia
- LinkedIn https://www.linkedin.com/in/gert-franz-4056807/
- Helsana https://www.helsana.ch/en/individuals

Episode:

- 004 <u>Performance Tuning and the Future of Lucee with Gert Franz</u>
- 024 <u>CFML Debugging Jedi Tricks and Templates, with Gert Franz</u>

Giancarlo Gomez

Giancarlo Gomez is a full-stack developer with over 17 years experience with various languages, technologies and a passion to continue to learn. He has been a designer, developer and project lead for several companies stateside and can even say this path took him across the pond years back for a piece of software he wrote that required installation and configuration. The internet was much slower back then and a flight was required. He is the owner/lead developer of Fuse Developments, Inc. (<u>http://www.fusedevelopments.com/</u>) established in 2004, his consulting business specializing in web and mobile development and CrossTrackr, Inc. (<u>https://crosstrackr.com/</u>), a SaaS for the CrossFit community, targeted towards athletes and gym owners providing real-time insight into athletic progress and health metrics.

Links:

- Website <u>http://giancarlogomez.com</u>
- CrossTrackr <u>https://crosstrackr.com/</u>
- Fuse Developments <u>http://www.fusedevelopments.com/</u>

Episode:

- 001 <u>Amazing Adventures with CF WebSockets with Giancarlo Gomez</u>

Grant Shepert

UK Branch Manager at Blue River Interactive Group

Links:

- Mura Digital Experience Platform <u>http://www.getmura.com/</u>
- Blue River <u>http://www.blueriver.com/</u>

Episode:

N/A

Guust Nieuwenhuis

Guust Nieuwenhuis is a freelance Senior Full Stack Web Developer with experience in a wide range of technologies. Over the last couple of years, he has been involved in projects for various clients like:

European Commission (https://ec.europa.eu/), NSHQ (NATO) (https://www.nshq.nato.int/), Adobe (https://www.adobe.com/), AS Adventure Group, NS (Dutch railways) (https://www.ns.nl/en), Proximus (https://www.proximus.be/en/id_personal/personal.html).

Recently Guust started developing his own product: Pedrillo. It's a SAAS solution for music orchestra's to manage their musicians, events, library, etc.

In his free time, Guust plays the double bass and drums/percussion, both in small ensembles as in symphony orchestra's. He likes spending as much time as possible with his family and meeting friends for a chat, game or drink. When he still has some time left, he mainly spends it behind his computer to fulfil his hunger for the latest trends in IT.

Links:

- Website http://guustnieuwenhuis.be/
- Twitter http://www.twitter.com/lagaffe
- LinkedIn http://be.linkedin.com/in/guustnieuwenhuis
- Stackoverflow http://stackoverflow.com/users/1654074/guust-nieuwenhuis
- SlideShare http://www.slideshare.net/guustnieuwenhuis

Episode:

- 048 CF Continuous Integration Plumbing with Bitbucket Pipelines with Guust Nieuwenhuis

Igor Ilyinsky

Igor is the founder of FirmWise (https://www.firmwise.net/), and has helped redesign over a hundred law firm websites. He is a Marketing Technologist, Entrepreneur and entertaining presenter focused on advancing Law Firms to the highest level of marketing technology automation... Igor's gift is knowing how to translate techy jargon into common sense English that anyone can understand; even battle hardened attorneys. His experience in web development for nearly the past two decades and his popularity as a speaker make him the quintessential authority on what trends to pursue and what fads to avoid. As the Founder of FirmWise, the only web hosting platform developed specifically for law firms, Igor has helped define the web presence for over 200 law firms, and continues to pioneer strategy for the industry.

Specialties: Expertise in Law Firm Marketing, Web Content Management, ColdFusion, Web Hosting, Web Design, Database Architecture, IT Management and Search Engine Optimization (SEO)

Worked with numerous programming languages (including: Basic, Fortran, Pascal, Modula3, C/C++, Visual Basic, Active Server Pages, Java, Java Server Pages, Enterprise Java Beans, JavaScript, Livewire [Server Side JavaScript], Perl, Php, SQL, TSQL, PL/SQL, ColdFusion, ActionScript, WML, WMLS, XML and WSDL) on multiple OS platforms.

Links:
- Twitter https://twitter.com/igorilyinsky?lang=en
- LinkedIn https://www.linkedin.com/in/igorilyinsky/
- FirmWise https://www.firmwise.net/

Episode:

- 075 Breaking out of your ColdFusion comfort zone (How to make CF mainstream) with Igor Ilyinsky

Jeffrey Kunkel

Jeffrey Kunkel is an in house web developer for Lightning New York (www.lightingnewyork.com). He has been developing for six years, and is excited to start contributing to the ColdFusion community at large.

Jeff has been living with anxiety, depression, and OCD for his entire career. He wants to take the lessons he's learned working around and with these conditions to better the workflow and productivity of his colleagues.

Links:

- Twitter https://www.twitter.com/nerdtastic91686

Episode:

- 072 Oh my GAD (General Anxiety Disorder) with Jeffrey Kunkel

John Farrar

John Farrar started programming in the late 70's on a Commodore PET. He served in the U.S.Navy and then met his wife during his reservist years. This was when the Amiga drove his computer interest for several years. Eventually, he became a web developer and in the later 90's he started using ColdFusion building dynamic websites.

With about twenty years of web development, John has become known for his work with jQuery (https://jquery.com/), Knockout (http://knockoutjs.com/) and Vue AJAX libraries (https://vuejsdevelopers.com/2017/08/28/vue-js-ajax-recipes/). Sustainable and profitable come together when the right technology is applied to the correct challenges. John enjoys focusing on a strategy that will bring impact without getting delayed by over-engineering.

Links:

- Twitter http://www.twitter.com/@sosensible
- Sos Apps https://www.sosapps.com

Episodes:

- 018 VUE More With Less, with John Farrar
- 078 Agile ColdFusion API Development (Amazing Postman, ColdBox and Agile secrets) with John Farrar

Jon Clausen

Jon Clausen hails from Grand Rapids, Michigan and has been developing CFML applications for over a decade. He was born and raised in South Dakota and attended SDSU and DePaul University. In 2004, after 14 years with a Fortune 100 company, he founded Silo (https://silowebworks.com/), a full-stack development and technology consulting firm in Grand Rapids, Michigan.

Jon has developed and written applications in CFML, Javascript, PHP, and Ruby in addition to dabbling in Java (https://www.java.com/), Python (https://www.python.org/),
Bash (https://en.wikipedia.org/wiki/Bash_(Unix_shell)),
Scala (https://www.scala-lang.org/) and
Clojure (https://clojure.org/).

He keeps current with both old and new database technologies including
SQL Server (https://en.wikipedia.org/wiki/Microsoft_SQL_Server),
MySQL (https://www.mysql.com/), MariaDB (https://mariadb.org/),
Oracle (https://www.oracle.com/index.html),
PostgreSQL (https://www.postgresql.org/),
Couchbase (https://www.couchbase.com/), and – his personal NoSQL favorite – MongoDB (https://www.mongodb.com/).

After hours, Jon enjoys theater, fishing for smallmouth bass on the Great Lakes, and chauffeuring his 12-year-old daughter back and forth to the horse stables.

He is pleased to represent Ortus Solutions (https://www.ortussolutions.com/) as a product evangelist for the Box products and is eternally grateful for tools like ColdBox (https://www.coldbox.org/) and
CommandBox
(https://www.ortussolutions.com/products/commandbox),
which continue to evolve and demonstrate a bright future for CFML development.

Links:

- Silo https://silowebworks.com/
- LinkedIn https://www.linkedin.com/in/jonclausen/

Episode:

- 011 Portable CFML with Cloud deployments, Microservices and REST with Jon Clausen

Jorge Reyes

Jorge is a passionate Industrial Engineer born in El Salvador with 7 years of experience managing projects. Business manager at Ortus Solutions, Corp. (https://www.ortussolutions.com/)

Links:

- Twitter https://twitter.com/@jreyben
- Ortus Solutions http://www.ortussolutions.com/

Episode:

- 052 CF Suicide, Depression, and Recovery with Jorge Reyes

Kai Koenig

Kai Koenig works as a Software Solutions Architect for Ventego Creative (http://ventego-creative.co.nz/) in Wellington, New Zealand. He co-founded the company with two partners and also the CTO of Zen Ex Machina, a startup in the fields of digital & user experience consultancy based out of Canberra in Australia.

Kai's work really comprises a mix of consulting, training, mentoring and actual development work using a range of technologies, common themes being Java, CFML, JavaScript, Android etc. He is well versed in Java and some other JVM-based languages like Clojure or Groovy and recently (re-)discovered the pleasure of writing software in Python and Go. Kotlin is his new language love though.

Links:

- LinkedIn https://www.linkedin.com/in/kaikoenig/

Episode:

- 050 Improve your CFML Code Quality (with some Cool Tools) with Kai Koenig

Kevin Jones

Kevin Jones is a Technical Solutions Architect at NGINX (https://www.nginx.com/), where he specializes in the integration and implementation of NGINX for various companies around the world. He has a strong background in infrastructure management, application monitoring, and troubleshooting.

Links:

- Blog https://www.nginx.com/blog/author/kjones/
- Twitter https://twitter.com/webopsx?lang=en

Episode:

- 014 NGINX: A Smart Middle Man Between Your App and Your Users, with Kevin Jones

Kirk Deis

Kirk Deis (pronounced "Daysss") is the CEO of two companies based in Newport Beach, California.Treehouse51.com

(https://www.treehouse51.com/)
(ad agency) & TheBugSquasher.com (https://thebugsquasher.com/)
(universal web app). He has been featured in Forbes, online
publications and other podcast shows.

Links:

- The Bug Squasher https://thebugsquasher.com/
- Treehouse 51 https://www.treehouse51.com/

Episode:

- 081 Better Bug Squashing (New Issue Tracking Tool) with Kirk Deis

Kishore Balakrishnan

Kishore Balakrishnan is a Senior Product Marketing Manager at
Adobe Systems (https://www.adobe.com/) with a Master Degree in
Computer Applications. At Adobe he has held roles of a Quality
Manager, Program Manager before becoming the Product Marketing
Manager. He enjoys being the 'voice of the customer' within the
organization, liaise with sales team to facilitate the selling process
and clearly communicate the why, what and when to the marketplace
for CF. He lives in Bangalore with his wife and kid. Kishore loves his
long runs and cooking.

Link:

- LinkedIn
  https://www.linkedin.com/in/kishore-balakrishnan-8170807

Episode:

- 058 All about the Adobe CF Summit East 2018 ColdFusion with Kishore Balakrishnan

Logan Mayville

Logan Mayville is a digital marketing consultant for Southwestern Consulting specializing in direct-response initiatives like lead generation and e-commerce. As a certified Facebook advertising buyer and content strategist, he believes in the power of digital marketing to transform companies in terms of marketing ROI, sales, and customer service. Based in Sacramento, CA, Logan enjoys various mountain-related activities when he's not helping grow businesses.

Links:

- Southwest Consulting
  http://www.southwesternconsulting.com/
- LinkedIn https://www.linkedin.com/in/lmayville/
- Twitter https://twitter.com/Mayvillain

Episode:

- 068 Marketing Dark Arts for ColdFusion developers (FB Advanced Audience Creation and Tracking) with Logan Mayville

Luis Majano

Luis Majano is a Computer Engineer born in El Salvador and is the president of Ortus Solutions (www.ortussolutions.com), a consulting firm specializing in web development, architecture and professional open source support and services. His background includes over 16 years of software development experience, architecture, and system design. He is the creator of the ColdBox Platform (www.coldbox.org), CommandBox CLI (www.ortussolutions.com/products/commandbox), ContentBox Modular CMS (www.ortussolutions.com/products/contentbox) and is an Adobe Community Professional.

Links

- Twitter https://twitter.com/@lmajano

Episodes:

- 012 Extreme Testing and Slaying the Dragons of ORM with Luis Majano
- 044 CommandBox + ForgeBox: ColdFusion Code, Package, Share, Go! with Luis Majano

Mark Drew

Mark Drew has been programming CFML since 1996, and even though he has had forays into Perl, ASP and PHP he is still loving every line of code he has crafted with CFML. His career has concentrated on eCommerce, Content Management and Application Scalability for various well known brands in the UK market such as Jaeger (https://github.com/jaegertracing),
Hackett (https://github.com/lexi-lambda/hackett), Hobbs, Dyson, B&W, Diesel amongst others.

Links:

- Twitter https://twitter.com/markdrew
- LinkedIn https://www.linkedin.com/in/mdrew
- CFML Slack https://cfml.slack.com/
- CMDHQ https://cmdhq.io/

Episodes:

- 035 Getting started fast with Docker, with Mark Drew
- 043 Let's get GraphQL! (Smart API access from CFML), with Mark Drew
- 074 Planning for CFML ISP disaster (Commandbox and Docker to the rescue) with Mark Drew

Mary Jo Sminkey

Mary Jo is a long-time ColdFusion developer, having worked with CF since the Allaire days, and for many years she authored and sold one of the most popular ecommerce platforms for the language, CFWebstore. Today she works for CFWebtools as a Senior Developer, continuing to support and build large ecommerce websites. In her spare time, she enjoys a wide variety of hobbies, including dog training and showing, sewing, knitting, board gaming, origami, handbell choir and other musical pursuits, and is a reviewer for Amazon products via their Vine program. She is a cancer survivor and suffers from fibromyalgia as well as various RSI issues from years of computer work so encourages young developers to pay attention to their ergonomics and learning how to ensure a healthy work environment. She enjoys cosplaying and attending conventions and runs a Facebook group for Cosplay with Disabilities which helps advocate and support people who cosplay with disabilities and the challenges that entails.

Links:

- CF Web Tools https://www.cfwebtools.com/
- Twitter https://twitter.com/mjsminkey
- Facebook https://www.facebook.com/maryjo.sminkey

Episode:

- 027 Advanced Error Handling Strategies for ColdFusion, Javascript and SQL with Mary Jo Sminkey

Matt Gifford

Matt Gifford is owner and primary primate at his own development consultancy company, monkehWorks Ltd. His work primarily focuses on building mobile apps and ColdFusion development, although he's such a geek he enjoys writing in a variety of languages.

He's a published author and presents at conferences and user groups on a variety of topics. As an Adobe Community Professional and Adobe User Group manager, Matt is a keen proponent for community resources and sharing knowledge.

He is the author of "Object-Oriented Programming in ColdFusion" and "PhoneGap Mobile Application Development Cookbook" and also contributes articles and tutorials to international industry magazines.

Links:

- monkehWorks Ltd http://www.monkehworks.com/
- Twitter https://twitter.com/coldfumonkeh?lang=en

Episode:
- 049 OAuth 2 for Me and You (Social Login Lowdown) with Matt Gifford

Matthew Clemente

Matthew is the Founding Partner of Season 4, LLC (https://season4.io/), a team of designers, programmers, and writers working in the legal industry. After studying English, he took the road less traveled and one day realized, much to his surprise, that he had become a developer. Matthew have been building with ColdFusion since MX 7, and the community has been amazing from the start.

He is a husband, father, and always trying to be better.

Links:

- Season 4 https://season4.io/
- Twitter https://twitter.com/mjclemente84
- GitHub https://github.com/mjclemente

Episode:

- 055 send.Better() – Giving ColdFusion Email a REST with Matthew Clemente

Mike Brunt

Mike Brunt was born in Northern England in 1948. It was a time of austerity for the British people who had rationing in place due to the effects of the Second World War. He pursued a management career in transportation equipment becoming Director of Excess Stock at British Leyland Truck and Bus. He moved to the USA in 1989 and eventually took up a career path in technology, coinciding with the emergence of the World Wide Web. Mike then became involved in Teleradiology working alongside Kodak, Lucent Technologies and GTE. Currently Mike is still deeply involved in technology, being a specialist in capacity planning and tuning for Java systems and he is becoming ever more involved with Blockchain and peer-to-peer based infrastructure.

In addition to his career path Mike is a composer and musical having been involved in the creation of 11 electronic music albums, Mike also paints with well over 100 paintings located in Los Angeles, New Zealand and Eugene Oregon. Lastly Mike is a Permaculture Certified Designer and lives on a 5 acre farm in the Eugene area of Oregon.

Mike Brunt is also known as CF Whisperer.

Links:

- Twitter https://twitter.com/cfwhisperer?lang=en
- FaceBook https://www.facebook.com/mike.brunt
- Instagram
  https://www.instagram.com/eugenepermaculture/
- CF Whisperer http://www.cfwhisperer.com/

- Java Mem http://www.javamem.com/
- JVM Services http://www.jvm.services/

Episodes:

- 009 Tuning & Troubleshooting ColdFusion Using Native Tools with Mike Brunt
- 082 ColdFusion and the Blockchain Revolution with Mike Brunt

Mike Collins

Senior ColdFusion consultant at SupportObjective (http://www.supportobjective.com/) providing development, services including applications, migration projects, and annual ColdFusion support. Mike started using ColdFusion during his time with Allaire (https://en.wikipedia.org/wiki/Allaire_Corporation), Macromedia (https://en.wikipedia.org/wiki/Macromedia), and Adobe (https://www.adobe.com/). Over the years Mike has given several ColdFusion conference sessions concerning developing and architecting ColdFusion applications.

Links:

- Support Objective http://www.supportobjective.com/

Episode:

- 062 Scaling Your ColdFusion Applications (Clusters, Containers and Load Tips) with Mike Collins

Miles Rausch

Miles Rausch is a web developer from Sioux Falls, South Dakota.

He is a writer for people, and a writer for computers. He believes that he is destined to spend his time at a keyboard.

During his work time, he develops for both server (in CFML using the Lucee engine) and client (where he tries to be unobtrusive, semantic and responsibly future-facing). At the same time, Miles have been having a flirty affair with Node.js and React.

In his personal time, he writes short stories and novels. Fiction is as strong a passion for Miles as programming, and he has published in some online publications and some print magazines.

Links:

- Website http://milesrausch.com/
- Twitter https://twitter.com/awayken
- LinkedIn https://linkedin.com/in/milesrausch

Episode:

- 057 Progressive Web Apps Building – Amazing Lucee CFML and ColdBox Tricks with Miles Rausch

Nathaniel Francis

Nathaniel Francis is an employee of Computer Know How (https://compknowhow.com/), the Wisconsin-based technology firm and ColdBox Alliance Partner (https://www.ortussolutions.com/blog/new-coldbox-alliance-partner-computer-know-how). He has been working with ColdBox (https://www.coldbox.org/) since he started at CKH in September of 2012. His focus is on ColdBox applications, ContentBox sites, and ColdBox REST apps. He is a husband, father of 8, worship leader, theologian, scifi enthusiast, and balding.

Links:

- Twitter https://twitter.com/@francainath
- Computer Know How http://compknowhow.com/

Episode:

- 008 The Best REST You've ever Had: ColdBox REST with Nathaniel Francis

Neil Cresswell

Neil is the co-founder of Portainer.io (https://portainer.io/), which is an open-source "human friendly" Management UI for Docker; the founder of CloudInovasi.id (https://cloudinovasi.id/), which is a Indonesia-centric Docker Container as a Service Provider (and which provided the initial inspiration for Portainer), and is the co-founder of a NZ company called Emerging Technology Partners, which specialises in Docker consulting.

Links:

- Portainer https://portainer.io/
- CloudInovasi https://cloudinovasi.id/

Episode:

- 064 Using Portainer.io (Docker Container Management) with Neil Cresswell

Nolan Erck

Chief consultant at South of Shasta (http://southofshasta.com/).

Nolan Erck has been developing software for 19 years. Starting in the video game industry working on titles for Maxis and LucasArts, then advancing to web development in 1999, his list of credits includes Grim Fandango, StarWars Rogue Squadron, SimPark, SimSafari as well as high-traffic websites for clients. Nolan manages the SacInteractive User Group, teaches classes on aspects of software development, and regularly gives presentations at conferences and user groups across the country.

Links:

- Twitter https://twitter.com/southofshasta
- GitHub https://github.com/nolanerck

Episodes:

- 005 Dependency Injection, why is it awesome and why should I care? with Nolan Erck
- 047 Best Practices Are Best, Except When They're Not with Nolan Erck
- 051 Git ColdFusion Source Control (Getting Started and Best Practices) with Nolan Erck
- 059 Migrating legacy CFML to MVC (Model View Controller) with Nolan Erck
- 069 Font Awesome and ColdFusion (never build icons again) with Nolan Erck

Patrick Quinn

CoFounder, CEO and CTO of Webapper. Global Product manager at LAS.

Patrick is the Co-Founder and CEO/CTO of Webapper Services (https://www.webapper.com/). Since 2001, he has been providing a true one-stop-shop consulting experience for customers with CFML-based web applications (ColdFusion or Lucee). His company worked on many of the largest, highest-traffic systems in this space. In recent years, with the advent of cloud technology, they have been able to transform into a new kind of hosting company, where they combine AWS's leading cloud technology with our extensive web application engineering expertise. The result is an even better experience for their customers, who benefit not only from a 21st-century "true cloud" hosting infrastructure, but also from dramatically improved tech support that's delivered by engineers who are not only well-versed (and certified) in AWS technology, but who are also experienced application engineers.

Patrick's strongest professional interest at this juncture of his career lies at the locus of culture, process, and code. In short, he thrives on the alchemy of combining these 3 key ingredients for creating high-performing technology organizations. He has personally delivered over 500 successful engagements, to hundreds of customers all over the world.

Patrick was born and raised in Chicago, received his bachelor's and master's degrees at The University of Chicago in the 1990s, and have been solving technology problems ever since.

Links:

- Webapper https://www.webapper.com/
- SeeFusion https://www.seefusion.com/
- LinkedIn https://www.linkedin.com/in/patrickmquinn/

Episode:

- 039 CFML Secrets with Patrick Quinn (AWS, Lucee and SeeFusion)

Pete Freitag

Pete Freitag has well over a dozen years of experience building web applications with ColdFusion. In 2006 he started Foundeo Inc (https://foundeo.com/), a ColdFusion consulting and products company. Pete helps clients develop and architect custom ColdFusion applications, as well as review and improve the performance and security of existing applications. He has also built several products and services for ColdFusion including a Web Application Firewall for ColdFusion called FuseGuard (https://foundeo.com/security/fuseguard/) and a ColdFusion server security scanning service called HackMyCF (https://hackmycf.com/). Pete holds a BS in Software Engineering from Clarkson University.

Links:

- Foundeo http://foundeo.com/
- Twitter http://www.twitter.com/pfreitag/
- Pete Freitag Website http://www.petefreitag.com/

Episode:

- 020 <u>Secrets of High-Security ColdFusion Code, With Pete Freitag</u>

Peter Ivanov

Peter Ivanov is Manager, Entrepreneur and Virtual teams Expert with over 20 years of international experience.

Born in Bulgaria he graduated Mathematics and joined a multinational company as Data Analyst. He quickly became IT Manager for Bulgaria and gradually worked his way up to IT Services Manager for Eastern Europe, Middle East and Africa. Peter recognized the growing importance of the teams in multiple locations and developed an innovative method for leading Virtual teams.

In 2007 the Team led by Peter won the "Best of the Best" award for outstanding Project management in establishing global Shared services.

In 2012 his Team won the "Global IT Connect Award" for excellent Engagement in a global cross-functional environment.

In 2013 Peter founded "Virtual Power Teams" and started new career as Keynote speaker and Executive coach on New Leadership.

Peter is a passionate athlete and World Senior Champion in Discus. He actively supports young Talents in the fields of mathematics and sports.

In his dynamic keynote speeches and master classes, held in English, German, Bulgarian and Russian, Peter uses the experience he has gained as Manager, Athlete, Entrepreneur and, yes, the father of five little girls, to show you how to build up and lead your own successful Virtual Teams.

As an expert in New Leadership Peter supports managers to retain the gravity of their Team despite the geographical distance, age and cultural differences, and deliver Top business performance!

Links:

- Virtual Power Teams http://www.peter-ivanov.com/

Episode:

- 060 Virtual Power Teams for ColdFusion Development (3 mistakes to avoid) with Peter Ivanov

Rakshith Naresh

Rakshith Naresh senior product manager for ColdFusion at Adobe (https://www.adobe.com/). He decides the future direction of CF there.

Links:

- LinkedIn https://www.linkedin.com/in/rakshith/

Episode:

- 042 Revealing the ColdFusion 2018 Roadmap details, with Rakshith Naresh

Sami Gardner

Sami Gardner is a Career Stagnation Stopper, Librarian, and World Traveler. She inspires technical, artistic, socially conscious types to craft their career on their terms. With experience in peer counseling, higher education, and facilitating career services at international tech bootcamps, she guides clients in evolving their careers.

Links:

- Sami Gardner http://www.samigardner.com/
- Facebook https://www.facebook.com/thesamigardner/
- LinkedIn https://www.linkedin.com/in/samigardner/

Episode:

- 038 Smart Developer Career Strategies and How Women Can Get Ahead in Tech with Sami Gardner

Samuel Knowlton

Founder and president of inLeague (http://www.inleague.org/), boutique ColdFusion software development house.

Links:

- InLeague http://www.inleague.org/

Episode:

- 061 The Great ColdFusion Entrepreneurial Adventure (from side jobs to freelancing to your own biz) with Samuel Knowlton

Saravanamuthu J

Founder & CTO at MitrahSoft

Links:

- MitrahSoft http://www.mitrahsoft.com/
- LinkedIn https://www.linkedin.com/in/cfmitrah/

Episode:

N/A

Scott Coldwell

Scott is a developer and sysadmin at Computer Know How (http://www.compknowhow.com/blog) and has been building the web since 2006. He loves elegant, simple solutions and helping others achieve the same.

Links:

- Twitter https://twitter.com/@scottcoldwell
- Computer Know How http://www.compknowhow.com/blog
- LinkedIn https://www.linkedin.com/in/scott-coldwell-0147a612/

Episode:

- 017 Managing an international team, Git, CFML, Node, Joomla, Headaches and Heartaches, with Scott Coldwell

Seth Engen

Seth Engen is a co-owner of Computer Know How (http://compknowhow.com/), a Wisconsin-based technology firm that he started with Curt Gratz in 1997. At the companies start he was introduced to CFML (version 4) and has been programming in the language ever since. Seth really enjoys creating web applications with great user interface experiences.

Links:

- Twitter https://twitter.com/@engens
- Computer Know How http://compknowhow.com/

Episode:

- 016 Adventures with ColdFusion and ContentBox in the Wild, with Seth Engen

Sophia Eng

Sophia Eng (http://www.sophiaeng.com/) is a tactical and intuitive growth advisor and consultant to women in startups and small businesses. She also holds the position of Senior Manager, Online Marketing at InVision App (http://www.invisionapp.com/). Views are her own.

Sophia has a passion for closing the minority and gender gap in business leadership and ownership. Recently, she founded a community group called Women in Growth (https://www.facebook.com/groups/779100078941215/), open to all women in startup, tech, and business communities for support.

Links:

- Hear Us Roar Manifesto https://thinkgrowth.org/hear-us-roar-a-manifesto-for-women-and-minorities-in-startup-tech-and-business-communities-f5b75be7c5b
- Sophia's Website http://sophiaeng.com/
- FB group women in growth https://www.facebook.com/groups/womengrow

Episode:

- 034 Hear Us Roar: A Manifesto for Women and Minorities in Startup, Tech, and Business Communities with Sophia Eng

Steven Hauer

Steven Hauer is currently the International Business Manager for Bridges for Peace. He is married to the love of his life Cheryl Hauer and living in Jerusalem, Israel. He likes to play the guitar. With his son Jared, he is instrumental in the development and evolution of dev.Objective().

Links:

- Facebook https://www.facebook.com/steven.hauer
- Twitter https://twitter.com/stevenhauer

Episode:

- 021 Behind the Scenes at CFObjective, with Steven Hauer

Steven Neiland

Originally from Cork Ireland, Steven Neiland currently works remotely out of Tampa Florida as a senior web developer at SiteVision Inc (https://sitevision.com/).

Links:

- LinkedIn http://www.neiland.net/
- Twitter https://twitter.com/sneiland
- GitHub https://github.com/sneiland

Episode:

- 031 Going Modular With Fw/1 Subsystems 2.0, with Steven Neiland

Sumit Verma

Sumit brings over 15 years of RIA, web development and technology management expertise to ten24 (https://www.ten24web.com/). He is directly responsible for overseeing the development process for each project and managing ten24's technical infrastructure. Sumit has successfully implemented projects calling on his diverse skills that involve: E-Commerce Applications, ERP Applications, CRM Applications, Client/Server Solutions, System Analysis & Architecture, Database Designing and Administration, for clients such as Working Advantage, Pongo Resume, Stonyfield Farms and White's Nursery.

Sumit also brings knowledge of core programming languages including: C, C++, COBOL, ColdFusion, Flex, PeopleSoft (Financials, HRMS), CRM (Siebel), Client / Server Solutions (Visual Basic) and Databases (Oracle, MS SQL Server, MySQL) using OOAD methodologies and modeling tools (Convoy DM, Rational).

Links:

- Ten24 https://www.ten24web.com/

Episode:

- 076 Slatwall ColdFusion eCommerce Unleashed (Beyond Shopping Carts) with Sumit Verma

Thomas Grobicki

CEO of Avilar Technologies, Inc (http://www.avilar.com/). talent management apps – learning and competency management system in hospital healthcare, insurance, finance, and DOD.

Links:

- Avilar http://www.avilar.com/
- LinkedIn https://www.linkedin.com/in/thomas-grobicki-3a90322/

Episode:

- 041 The true ROI of ColdFusion (How to Sell CF to your Boss or Client) with Thomas Grobicki

Tridib Roy Chowdhury

Tridib Roy Chowdhury is the G.M. and Sr. Director of Products at Adobe Systems (https://www.adobe.com/) and is responsible for ColdFusion.

Over the last 10 years at Adobe, he has built a global team consisting of engineers, product and data architects, product managers, product marketers, experience designers and sales.

Tridib has been driving data-driven decision making much before it was fashionable.

Links:

- LinkedIn https://www.linkedin.com/in/tridib-roy-chowdhury-b744893/

Episode:

- 065 The Future of ColdFusion (it is Bright) with Tridib Roy Chowdhury

Uma Ghotikar

Uma Ghotikar has more than 6 years of experience in web application development, database design and development. She has a technical educational background. She did Master of Science in Information Systems from George Mason University, USA and Bachelor of Engineering in Information Technology from University of Mumbai, India. She enjoys coding especially the back-end development and learning new technical skills.

Links:

- ICF https://www.icf.com/
- LinkedIn https://www.linkedin.com/in/umaghotikar/
- Twitter https://twitter.com/umaghotikar

Episode:

- 077 Fundamentals of Unit Testing, BDD and Mocking (using TestBox and MockBox) with Uma Ghotikar

APPENDIX B

Resources

"Learning teacheth more in one year than experience in twenty." -
Roger Ascham, Writer

Links

You can find all the linked podcasts, articles and tools from this book
at: www.teratech.com/CFAliveBookLinks

CF Alive Podcast

You can find over 80 episodes of the CF Alive podcast podcast at

- www.teratech.com/podcast

Hear CF experts, bloggers and CIOs interviewed about how they use
modern ColdFusion.

Books
- "The Inevitable: Understanding the 12 Technological Forces
  That Will Shape Our Future" by Kevin Kelly
- "The End of Jobs: Money, Meaning and Freedom Without the
  9-to-5" by Taylor Pearson
- The 80/20 Principle: The Secret to Achieving More with Less
  by Richard Koch

Gratitudes

I am grateful to the following people who helped in creating this book.

- Book details
  - Editing: El Princess Eclar and Paul Zivotic
  - Copy Editor: Joyce Simpson
  - Writing help: Bobby Bernal
  - Marketing: Judy Schramm and Paul Zivotic
  - Executive Assistant: El Princess Eclar
  - Photographer: Sean Dalton
  - Cover design: Design Pickle https://www.designpickle.com/ and Pixel Studio www.fiverr.com/pixelstudio/design-a-professional-book-cover
  - Kindle and Create Space formatting Tnkopfk www.fiverr.com/tnkopfk/professionally-format-and-convert-to-kindle-format
  - Sound Engineers: Christopher Lang, El Princess Eclar and Paul Zivotic

- All the beta readers:
  - Angel Christian Torres, Gert Franz, Jorge Reyes, Judy Schramm, Kishore Balakrishnan, Lorenzo Swank, Mark Drew, Mike Brunt, Miles Rausch, Nolan Erck, Pavle Zivotic, Pete Freitag and Robin Wolfson.

- Everyone who has attended MDCFUG, CFUnited, CF_Underground, MiniMax, Frameworks conferences and our ColdFusion classes and webinars over the years.

- All the interviewees for the <u>CF Alive podcast</u>:
  - Alex Skinner, April Graves, Bouton Jones, Brad Wood, Brad, Luis and Gavin combo , Bret Fisher, Brian Klaas, Brian Sappey, Carol Hamilton, Charlie Arehart, Christine Ballisty, David Tattersall, Dominic Watson, Ed Bartram,

Elishia Dvorak, Elliotte Bowerman, Eric Peterson, Esmeralda Acevedo, Gavin Pickin, Geoff Bowers , George Murphy, Gert Franz, Giancarlo Gomez, Guust Nieuwenhuis, Igor Ilyinsky, Jeffrey Kunkel, John Farrar, Jon Clausen, Jorge Reyes, Kai Koenig, Kevin Jones, Kirk Deis, Kishore Balakrishnan, Logan Mayville, Luis Majano, Mark Drew, Mary Jo Sminkey, Matt Gifford, Matthew Clemente, Mike Brunt, Mike Collins, Miles Rausch, Nathaniel Francis, Neil Cresswell, Nolan Erck, Patrick Quinn, Pete Freitag, Peter Ivanov, Rakshith Naresh, Raymond Camden, Sami Gardner, Samuel Knowlton, Scott Coldwell, Seth Engen, Sophia Eng, Steven Hauer, Steven Neiland, Sumit Verma, Thomas Grobicki , Tridib Roy Chowdhury, Uma Ghotikar.

A Personal Note
from Michaela Light

I hope you've enjoyed this CF Alive book. You probably know how important reviews are to the success of a book on Amazon or Kindle. If you've enjoyed this book, then I'd be very grateful if you could post a review on www.amazon.com or www.amazon.co.uk or your local Amazon website.

Your comments do really matter and I read all reviews since readers' feedback encourages me to keep experimenting and writing about business intuition. If you'd like to leave a review, then all you have to do is go to the review section on the "CF Alive" Amazon page. Scroll down from the top and under the heading of "Customer Reviews" and you'll see a big button that says "Write a customer review."

5. Scroll down the page until you see the "customer reviews" section. Click the button.

– click that and you're ready to get into action. You don't need to write much – a sentence or two is enough, essentially what you'd tell a friend or family member about the book.

Remember to leave

- A number of stars out of 5
- A review
- A title for the review
- … and don't forget to hit "submit".

Thanks again for your support!

You can learn more about the CF Alive revolution and more modern CF tools our website www.teratech.com. There you can follow our ColdFusion blog and podcast.

Yours abundantly,
Michaela Light

Want More?

Keep up with the latest CF methods and news on the TeraTech website blog and podcast.

Happy CFing!
Michaela Light

Made in the USA
Monee, IL
18 March 2022

93106288R00125